# Simple Greenhouse Gardening

## OTHER CONCORDE GARDENING BOOKS

# Simple Greenhouse Gardening

Edited by
Roger Grounds

WARD LOCK LIMITED·LONDON

© WARD LOCK LIMITED 1972

Casebound ISBN 0 7063 1329 1
Paperbound ISBN 0 7063 1128 0

First published in Great Britain 1972
by Ward Lock Limited, 116 Baker Street,
London, W1M 2BB
Reprinted 1976

Text in Baskerville (169/312)

Filmset and printed in England by
Cox and Wyman Ltd
London, Fakenham and Reading

# Contents

# Preface

Most books about greenhouse gardening assume from the outset that the reader is already an accomplished gardener, familiar with the techniques of gardening, and that he already possesses all the knowledge contained in its pages before he has read the first chapter. The facts are often very different. This book, almost perversely, assumes that the reader knows practically nothing about greenhouses or gardening and takes him step by step through the stages of choosing a greenhouse, selecting a site, laying the foundations, putting it up, lighting it, heating it and maintaining it, and then goes on to describe the wealth of plants, fruits and vegetables that can be grown in the greenhouse, together with details of their temperature requirements and cultivation.

*Simple Greenhouse Gardening* contains, in simple lucid terms, all the information an amateur needs to run a greenhouse with the minimum of effort and maximum of pleasure and satisfaction.

Roger Grounds

◀ Tomato, 'Sutton's Sorrento Cross', one of the best varieties for the amateur's greenhouse. It is exceptionally heavy-cropping, bears very large fruits, and is one of the new disease-resistant race of tomatoes. *Courtesy of Sutton's Seeds.*

# 1 Greenhouse Structure and Design

**Introducing the greenhouse – construction materials – greenhouse shape – selecting a site – foundations and erection – maintenance – heating – ventilation and shading**

A greenhouse adds a new dimension to a garden. In it you can grow a range of exotic flowering plants, fruits and vegetables that would simply perish out-of-doors in the ill-mannered winters of a temperate climate. And it does not require a lot of time or expertise to get a great deal of fun out of a greenhouse.

Once he has a greenhouse, a gardener can decide whether he is going to use it for growing exotic, tropical blooms, for forcing bulbs, raising cuttings, seedlings and summer bedding plants, or for growing tomatoes, melons, cucumbers, grapes and other luscious fruits and vegetables. However, since there is a relationship between the type of greenhouse you buy and the sort of crops you can cultivate in it, the first question to be considered is what type of greenhouse you want. There are two ways to tackle this problem: either work out what sort of plants you want to grow and select a greenhouse suitable for the purpose, or decide what you can afford and choose – as most people do – the best-value model in your price range.

8

Despite its mysterious reputation, greenhouse gardening is not difficult. There are no secrets to success. All you need in order to run a greenhouse that will give you the greatest pleasure for the least effort is to decide what you want to do, to find out the right way to do it, then do it.

A temperate climate, such as that of the British Isles, has many advantages to offer the outdoor gardener, but it also has its draw-backs: the majority of plants raised in the open have a growing season which lasts for little more than five of the twelve months of the year. Even then, the bulk of outdoor flowers bloom in the first three months of the summer, while most of the fruit crop is produced in its last two months. Some garden plants, it is true, will flower in winter out-of-doors, but they are few in number, far from diverse, and the vagaries of the weather are such that they are not always very successful.

A greenhouse ameliorates the intemperance of the weather, and enables you to grow special plants. Just how special these plants may be depends precisely on the lengths you are prepared to go to in controlling the climate within the greenhouse. This, in turn, is largely determined by what you are prepared, or are able to spend on both the greenhouse itself and on heating it. Plainly, the greater the degree of control you wish to exercise over the greenhouse's internal atmosphere, the more it will cost you.

Basically, there are four sorts of greenhouse to choose from, each maintained at a different temperature:

**Cold greenhouses** are heated solely by the sun. Although this restricts the house's usefulness to spring, summer and autumn, the results you get will depend a lot on where you live. Success will be greatest in sheltered, southerly spots, but even there the greenhouse will, except in abnormally mild winters, be useless for overwintering any plants which aren't hardy.

**Cool greenhouses** fit the needs and the pockets of many amateur gardeners. Unheated in summer, they are warmed artificially from autumn to spring to keep the temperature steady at about 45 °F. Being frost-free, the cool house is ideal for overwintering non-hardy plants, dahlia tubers and other garden stock. During summer the greenhouse can be filled with crops like tomatoes that can be difficult to grow out-of-doors.

9

Coleus. These plants are grown for their colourful leaves, which are more brightly coloured than the flowers of many other plants. They are easily raised from seeds or cuttings.

**Intermediate or warm houses** are kept at a heat never less than 55 °F. This means that they will raise tomatoes, cucumbers and other crops, both winter and summer; are excellent for growing pot plants, and for propagation.

**Stove or hot houses**, used for growing several kinds of orchids, tender plants, palms and for high-temperature propagation, are heated so that they stay over 65 °F.

Depending on the temperature, therefore, you will be able to grow a wide range of plants, shown in the table opposite. The cultivation of many of them is discussed in more detail in the second part of the book, but it is obvious that you do not, for example, need a hot house to grow orchids or even intermediate temperatures to be successful with melons and grapes.

| COOL | INTERMEDIATE | HOT |
|------|--------------|-----|
| Agapanthus | Adiantum | Aristolochia |
| Asparagus | Asplenium | Orchid |
| Azalea | Aubergine | Palms |
| Cacti | Begonia | Pineapple |
| Chrysanthemum | Bougainvillea | |
| Cucumber | Carnation | |
| Cyclamen | Chrysanthemum | |
| French bean | Cucumber | |
| Fuchsia | Freesia | |
| Lettuce | Gloxinia | |
| Marrow | Hyacinth | |
| Melon | Lettuce | |
| Mint | Mustard and cress | |
| Orchid | Nectarine | |
| Rhubarb | Orchid | |
| Sea Kale | Peach | |
| Tomato | Saintpaulia | |
| | Strawberry | |
| | Tomato | |
| | Vines | |

## Construction materials

Before you buy a greenhouse, send off for all the brochures you can and read them thoroughly. You will then be in a good position to browse round a garden centre or flower show before making a final choice. Remember that the more glass there is in the greenhouse in relation to solid materials, especially when there are no brick or composition base walls, the more heat the house will lose when there is no sunshine. This means that it is more expensive to keep an 'all glass' greenhouse at the temperature you want, than it is to keep a greenhouse with brick half-walls at the desired temperature.

The vast majority of modern greenhouses are manufactured in prefabricated sections though there is nothing to prevent a do-it-yourself enthusiast from building from scratch. How easy they are to erect depends on the detailed design, so it is well worth finding out in advance the time and trouble that will be involved in putting up a greenhouse of any particular type. The leading manufacturers deliver the complete greenhouse in sections anywhere in Britain and supply detailed erection instructions. When ordering a greenhouse, give the manufacturers clear, precise instructions.

Aluminium alloy, western red cedar, pressure-treated softwoods, and galvanized or enamelled steel are the most common materials used for the framework of the greenhouse. They will need little or no maintenance. Many designs use putty for internal glazing with external glassings. Alternatively, some designs use dry glazing, which involves sliding the glass into grooves, or clip-glaze by using metal clips to fit the glass on to a seal of plastic beading or bitumen. The following table gives a good idea of the features of various greenhouse materials.

| MATERIAL | STRENGTH/ BULK RATIO | COST | DURABILITY |
|---|---|---|---|
| Redwood | Medium | Low | Good if painted or treated |
| Steel | Very high | Low | Rusts unless galvanised or painted regularly |
| Pressure-treated softwoods | Variable | Low | Good |
| Red Cedar | Low | Medium | Good |
| Cast iron | Medium/high | Medium | Less liable to rust than steel |
| Reinforced concrete | Low | Medium | Good |
| Aluminium alloy | High | Medium | Believed good |
| Imported hardwood | Medium | High | Good |
| Burma teak | High | High | Very good |
| Oak | High | High | Good |

Light is all-important to plant growth and this is especially true of greenhouse plants, many of which come from very sunny climates. Because light is so vital, take the trouble to ensure the best possible ratio between glass and framework in the greenhouse – but bear heating costs in mind.

## Greenhouse shape

The shape of your greenhouse will have an effect on the amount of light and heat reaching the plants within, particu-

Mini and Maxi. Two extremes in size of greenhouses. 1. is the Hall's Mini Greenhouse in red cedar. 2. is a commercial greenhouse.

larly in Britain where the angle at which the sun's rays strike the ground – the angle of incidence – varies widely from summer through to winter. Although in the north of the country the days are longer in summer, the angle of incidence is smaller and the sun's rays less powerful. The more acute the angle of incidence, the less efficient your greenhouse will be, for the nearer the angle of incidence is to 90°, the more light and heat will get into the greenhouse.

A greenhouse with a conventional tent-shaped sloping roof will absorb light differently in different positions. If the length

| GREENHOUSE TYPE | SPECIAL FEATURES | RANGE OF ACTIVITIES |
| --- | --- | --- |
| SPAN-ROOFED (wood, alloy, steel, concrete) | Brick base wall | Pot plants, propagation, chrysanthemums in pots. |
| | Weatherboard base wall | Retain less heat, but base wall can be lined with insulating materials such as fibre glass. |
| | Glass to ground level | More costly to heat, but better light transmission makes them ideal for ground-grown crops. |
| LEAN-TO (Single pitch or ¾-span) | With or without base wall | Will grow most crops, but there can be problems with ventilation and overheating unless extractor fans are installed. Light distribution unequal. Excellent for peaches etc. against wall. |
| DUTCH LIGHT | Static | Ideal for summer crops. Frequently used for lettuce and tomatoes. Much heat loss from loose glazing system. |
| | Mobile | Allows a system of crop rotation which can be very useful. |
| CURVILINEAR | On small base wall or with glass to ground level | Both ideal for most activities. Heat loss fairly high with second type. |
| CIRCULAR | Still in fairly early stages of development | Particularly good for pot plant culture and propagation. Fan ventilation or 'air conditioning' is likely to be beneficial. |
| PLASTIC | 'Do-it-yourself' type | Will grow most crops provided crop support is adequate. Fan ventilation essential. |
| | Sophisticated type | Excellent for all activities, with added advantages of mobility. Fan ventilation is still essential. |

Portulaca are easily raised from seed in the greenhouse for planting out in spring.

Gladioli can be had in flower out of season when grown in the border of a cool greenhouse.

of the greenhouse runs east–west, during winter most of the sunlight will be deflected off the roof and absorbed through the vertical side walls. Once the sun gets higher in the sky, the south-facing slope of the roof will absorb radiation direct. Although sunlight will reach the back of the house, this does mean that a dense crop of plants on the south side of the greenhouse will shade any plants behind.

15

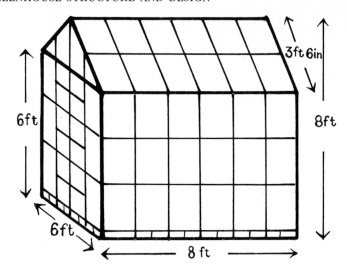

3ft 6in

6ft

8ft

6ft

8 ft

▲
Diagram showing how to calculate the area of glass through which heat is lost. Such calculations are necessary in order to find out how much heat needs to be put into the greenhouse to maintain any given minimum winter temperature.

Diagram showing how a large proportion of the sun's rays are deflected by the ▶ upper slope of a conventional span-roofed greenhouse.

Turning the greenhouse so that it faces north–south will even out the light in summer but has the disadvantage that in winter only the south-facing gable can catch the light. An east–west set-up will probably suit most gardeners best on balance, particularly if they use the greenhouse in winter, but it might be even more practical to select one of the new greenhouse designs with a semi-circular curved roof (a curvilinear greenhouse) or one completely circular in shape. These greenhouses, the results of experiments to find the best design for absorbing winter sun, function well all the year round when lined up east–west.

Experts often classify greenhouses according to the shape of their roofs:

**Span-roofed houses**, the most popular kind, are tent-shaped and have sides which are either vertical or slightly sloping. The roof rises to a ridge in the centre. The angle of the

roof varies widely, but the slope is generally steeper when the panes of glass overlap than when they do not. If you live in a place which gets a lot of snow in winter, choose a more sloping roof. This will help avoid damage, especially if the house is unheated.

The size of a span-roofed greenhouse can vary from 6 ft. × 4 ft. upwards, but the most popular size is 6 ft. × 8 ft., as this leaves room inside for two 3-ft. benches and a 2-ft. path or for two good-sized growing borders. The greenhouse glass can come right down to the level of the foundations, or the vertical walls may be built up for 2–3 ft. with brick or composition block. Or these base walls can be of metal, plastic, wood or asbestos. Some greenhouses have a base wall on one side and a glass front on the other, usually the south side, which is often an ideal compromise.

Gutters or eaves traverse the span-roofed greenhouse at

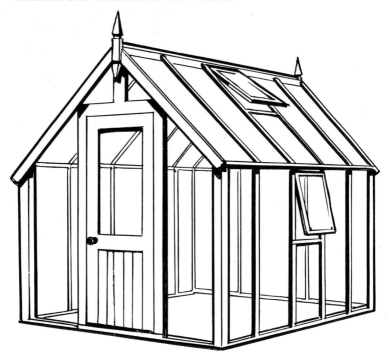

*Types of Greenhouse*
The traditional span-roofed type. This is the most popular of all greenhouse designs. It has been tried and tested over a long period of time and can be relied upon to give good all-round performance.

between 4 and 6 ft., while the ridge itself is usually some 2–3 ft. higher. The roof is fitted with ventilators, and sometimes the sides, too, though these side vents are unnecessary if you decide to fit the greenhouse with an extractor fan. In this case, ventilators need only serve as air inlets.

**Lean-to houses**, unpopular in the past because they were difficult to ventilate, became overheated in summer and trapped little light in winter, are modern favourites because they are convenient to use and can be heated direct from the domestic heating circuit, particularly if house and greenhouse are built at the same time. New fan designs have solved the ventilation difficulties, and the lean-to house can be very

Lean-to greenhouse or conservatory. Greenhouses of this type are economical to run, since heating can often be taken off the domestic supply. They are ideal where one wants to grow a vine up the back wall.

Dutch type greenhouse. This type of greenhouse is best used for growing plants in borders inside the greenhouse, and is particularly useful for growing tomatoes, winter lettuces, chrysanthemums and other plants not happy in pots.

Angle of incidence of the sun's rays in summer. Note the high proportion of rays actually reaching the floor of the greenhouse.

successful if situated facing south. If it faces west, then you might do best to employ it as a conservatory to catch the evening sun, while a north-facing lean-to is ideal for raising ferns, and some alpines and shade-loving pot plants.

The roof of the lean-to can either be a single slope or a three-quarter pitch with a ridge. Unless you can use the extra height of a ridge to fit an additional ventilator above the top level of the back wall, and level with one on the opposite slope, it is probably not worth the extra expense. If you cannot afford extractor fans, make sure that the ventilators on sides and front of any lean-to give a good through-current of air. The construction of lean-to greenhouses is very similar to that of span-roofed shapes.

**Porches**, like lean-to greenhouses, can be very useful, particularly for growing pot plants. Their greatest disadvantage is that they tend to be draughty, so that plants are chilled as doors are constantly opened and shut.

**Dutch light houses.** Although greenhouses with glass reaching to ground level are often called 'Dutch type', a true Dutch light greenhouse consists of single sheets of glass, each framed lightly in wood and measuring 5 ft. $\times$ $2\frac{1}{2}$ ft., which are then bracketed together by their grooved sides. The gable ends are hinged so that they can be lifted to make room for a tall crop. Popular with lettuce, tomato and chrysanthemum growers, these greenhouses are not such a good proposition for an amateur because their all-glass composition means a large heat loss and because warmth is also lost from between the frames which have to be held loosely in place to prevent damage from the wind. But Dutch light greenhouses are cheap to buy and very easy to put up.

An average single-span Dutch light greenhouse will measure 12–13 ft. in width and about 8 ft. in height. The low roof does restrict head and working room, but it is possible to build the whole house on to a brick base wall. Another modification used by professionals is to fit the greenhouse with pulley wheels so that it is mobile.

Dutch light greenhouses on wheels are especially useful for simple rotation of crops. As a first experiment, you could use one to cover an early crop of lettuce until March or the first weeks of April, push it along to be a sun-trap over a tomato crop in summer and finally use it as a house for chrysanthemums in an adjacent plot which had been planted in May. The next year, the plants could be changed round so that each has a new site. However, mobility will add an extra 25 or 30 per cent to the cost of a greenhouse which will already be expensive to heat and which takes up a lot of space.

**Curvilinear or Mansard houses**, because they allow so much light to enter, make ideal all-purpose greenhouses. A house of this shape would be an excellent choice if you wanted to specialize in pot plants and propagation. Made of alloy or treated steel, they are extremely sturdy and are obtainable in many different sizes and in lean-to form.

**Circular houses** have only recently become available, but

The staging arrangements in the 'Circulair' greenhouse. Note that there are three levels of staging. Those plants needing most light can be grown on the highest level of staging, whilst those needing least light can be grown on the lowest level. *Courtesy of Humex.*

The heating cables of the 'Circulair' greenhouse provide for all-round warmth and ensure an even temperature in all parts of the greenhouse. *Courtesy of Humex.*

The geodetic greenhouse, still regarded by some as a gimmicky novelty, is in fact designed on the soundest scientific principles. *Courtesy of 'Solardomes'.*

are rapidly growing in popularity as their efficiency is being broadcast. A built-in air-conditioning system or extractor fans are, however, a must, to prevent overheating in summer.

**Plastic greenhouses**, made of 500- or 1,000-gauge polythene or P.V.C. with rigid plastic supports, though not ideal, are cheap, simple to construct, can be moved around the garden, and are improving in design every year. Plastic greenhouses come in many different shapes and sizes; some, though rather flimsy, are designed so that you can build them yourself, while other, more sturdy types are obtainable ready made. The most recent model is the 'bubble' house which is inflated with one fan and ventilated with another.

A greenhouse made of thin plastic will probably last little more than two years. Eventually, the ultra-violet rays from the sun weaken the material and it is torn by the wind. Another disadvantage is that the plastic quickly becomes cloudy and dirty because dust clings to it very tightly. Although a plastic greenhouse will transmit light very efficiently, it will not, unlike a glass one, trap heat from the soil and from metal fittings, which means that it cools down very quickly. P.V.C., however, is slightly more effective than polythene.

Inside a plastic greenhouse, ventilation with electrically-powered fans is essential to cut down condensation, and this will, of course, add to the cost. Remember to anchor the greenhouse firmly and provide extra support for crops like tomatoes or cucumbers which are strung up against the walls.

Whatever their design, all greenhouses should be stable enough to withstand really strong winds and constructed so that the panes of glass do not vibrate and shatter. When making your choice, see that the greenhouse door is conveniently placed and wide enough to take a wheelbarrow, and that it opens inwards or slides back and forth. Try not to buy a house so small that you always have to stoop when inside. Small houses can be raised by placing them on three courses of bricks.

## Selecting a site

The success of your greenhouse will depend a great deal on where you put it, for a convenient spot in the garden will be useless if it gets no sun. Your aim should be a position which receives the maximum amount of sunshine both summer and winter – but remember to take into account the shade cast by trees and buildings, and for the variation in the angle of incidence of the sun's rays from June to December.

A perfect greenhouse site will be well sheltered, but the shelter will not cut down the light. Shelter is important because it cuts down the risk of damage from storms; it also cuts down heat loss. You will probably have to compromise between the protection it gives and a loss of sun for a short time each day. In very exposed areas, try to put the greenhouse between hedges running due north and south, as this will give good exposure to the midday sun. Although you will lose some light in the morning and the evening, the greenhouse will be sheltered from easterly and south-westerly gales.

Keep the greenhouse at least 10–15 ft. from a hedge to avoid overshading and interference from root growth. If trees are your shelter – like deciduous hedges they let light through in winter – double the distance. Solid walls are not a good idea: they stop the wind too sharply, deflecting it instead of breaking its force. Instead, choose an open fence, plastic mesh or 'lattice' wall.

Three other vital factors in selecting a site for your greenhouse are water, drainage and electricity. A good supply of water near at hand is essential, but you will have to obtain official permission from the local water board to fit a permanent water supply from the house, and be prepared to pay an increased water rate. If you do decide on this system, lay the permanent pipe underground to prevent freezing. Although you may be able to lay plastic pipes yourself, the job is probably best left to a qualified plumber.

Alternatives to a permanent pipe are the hose and the watering can, or an underground pipe fixed temporarily to an outside tap in, say, a garage. For the first of these methods, you will need a wide pipe, especially if you plan to use a spray or mist in the greenhouse as these need a good volume and pressure of water – about 40–60 lb. per sq. in. The second, temporary connection, is tolerated by most water boards, but does have the problem that water left in the pipes during winter may freeze and rupture the pipes.

Drainage is an aspect of greenhouse planning which is often ignored. A large amount of rain water will collect in the gutters or run off the roof of a greenhouse. If the greenhouse has gutters linked to vertical pipes, connect these to a drain or to a seep hole, which is a gravel-filled drainage pit. Should the rain run straight on to the ground around the greenhouse, lay tile or rubble drains joining up with a convenient field drain outlet or seep hole. A barrel will collect a significant amount of rain water which you can use to advantage in other parts of the garden.

When planning your electricity supply, look forward to the equipment you may acquire in future years. A light will use 100 watts of electric power, a heater $2\frac{1}{2}$ kilowatts. Added to a soil warming cable and possibly a mist irrigation unit, the total may be 4 or 5 kW., which will mean you will need a heavy-gauge electric cable. All electrical fittings and cable laying should be left to a qualified electrician, though you can do some of the preliminary work yourself.

Once you have laid your own greenhouse plans, don't forget that you may need planning permission from your local authority. This planning permission is usually necessary for a greenhouse more than 6 ft. × 8 ft., although regulations vary from area to area. To be on the safe side, it is worth submitting

Saintpaulias or African Violets are amongst the most popular of house plants. They can be grown in the greenhouse and taken indoors when in flower.

a scale plan, with the greenhouse position clearly marked in red, details of the dimensions (the manufacturer will supply plans, but you will have to draw these yourself if you are building your own greenhouse), and plans of the drains if they link up with main ducts. To support your application, the written acceptance of landlord or neighbours is a good idea, along with any special aspects of your greenhouse design such as attachment to the house.

A flat piece of land is, of course, the best place to start building a greenhouse, but it is well worth making the effort to level sloping ground thoroughly, particularly if you want to use the top-soil to make borders inside the house. The easiest time to level is when the soil is dry, and this will prevent damaging its texture, and you can choose one of the following three methods.

**Cut and fill.** In this process, the top-soil is stripped from the site and stacked on one side. The site is levelled by moving the sub-soil from the highest point to the lowest, then the top-soil is replaced. This simple procedure is excellent for a shallow slope, but on steeper ground you will run into drainage problems unless you build a retaining wall with a drain behind it to collect water running down from the higher ground.

If the top-soil is deep, you may not need to remove it, but whatever your method, do not be impatient. Wait for the soil to subside before you lay the greenhouse foundations. It is usually best to leave the soil for a whole winter to settle.

**Levelling to the lowest point** involves stripping off the top-soil, stacking it, removing the sub-soil to the level you want, then putting back the top-soil. While it is simple, this method can lead to drainage problems.

**Levelling to the highest point** is perhaps the best procedure, especially if the slope is acute, as it will solve most of your drainage difficulties. Use soil or ballast, depending on whether you want greenhouse borders, to raise the level. Add a wall at the base of the platform to keep the soil in place. The only disadvantage of this system is that drainage may be *too* efficient, and water run too quickly from the borders. This is because the greenhouse is largely above the normal soil level.

## Foundations and erection

The next step is to lay the greenhouse foundations, but before doing this you will need accurate measurements of the greenhouse. To avoid frustration, do wait until the greenhouse arrives, although delivery may take some weeks. Do not clutter up the site, but ask for the sections to be off-loaded near by. Then check the plans carefully, make sure that all the parts that should have been delivered have, in fact, been delivered, and verify all the measurements, noting whether they are 'outside to outside', 'inside to inside' or 'centre to centre'.

Now peg out the exact position of the greenhouse. Rather than using odd pieces of cane, take the trouble to cut inch-square wooden pegs, 14–16 in. long and pointed at one end.

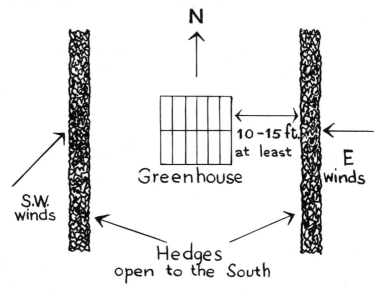

Diagram showing the siting of the greenhouse in relation to the points of the compass, to prevailing winds and to shelter belts.

Set one peg at the correct distance from fence, house or other landmark and then, using a good-quality steel measuring tape, put the other end peg in position, also at the right distance away from the landmark so that the greenhouse is in line. You can use a compass to check the orientation of the greenhouse, though it may not matter if you are a few degrees away from direct north–south or east–west.

To ensure accuracy, measure from the centre of each peg and set the end pegs in exact positions, adding intermediate ones if the greenhouse is very long, kept in line by means of a tightly-stretched cord. For a small greenhouse, a spirit level and a long straight board will be quite sufficient to check the horizontal level. A large house may need more sophisticated Cowley or 'Dumpy' level, but you may require expert help to use this instrument.

Now comes the difficult task of setting the width of the greenhouse at exact right-angles to the length. The easiest way to do this is to make up an accurate triangle with pieces of

An exterior view of an all-glass greenhouse. Note how the brickwork has been used to create a level plinth for the greenhouse structure.

wood 3, 4 and 5 ft. long, checking the right-angle formed with a joiner's square. Set the corner of this exactly to the nail and support the other two corners with bricks. Using two lines attached to the nail, form a right-angle along the edges of the triangle. Measure along the lines until you have the right width, and insert stakes. Check that the lengthwise distance is still correct, level up all the pegs and tap a nail into the centre of each corner peg. If you have a builder's site square, this will make really accurate right-angles, though again you may need expert help to use it.

Finally, attach taut lines to the nails on each corner peg. This can be done by placing stout pegs 2–3 ft. outside the outline of the greenhouse. Then remove the corner pegs. By doing this, you will leave yourself plenty of room for manœuvre, and the foundations can be worked without detracting from your accurate start and without having to work round the pegs.

The greenhouse supplier will tell you what sort of foundations you need to support a base wall or base blocks. Laying

29

A sequence showing construction of the greenhouse from beginning to end. Note that a level site is needed before construction can begin.

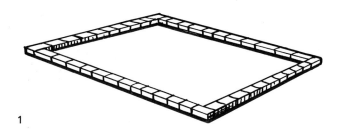

1

2

3

4

5

6

foundations should prove no problem to the do-it-yourself expert, but it is important to bear in mind that firm anchorage to the ground is essential.

Using the outside dimensions of the greenhouse as your guide, marked out with lines, dig a trench 5–6 in. deep and 12–14 in. wide if you are building a full 9-in. width brick wall, 8–9 in. wide if you plan a half-brick ($4\frac{1}{2}$-in.) wall or are using base or composition blocks. If you have just levelled the soil, you may need to dig deeper to find undisturbed ground.

Mix the concrete for the foundations using three parts finely-broken brick, two parts rough sand and one part cement. Run this in as a layer at least 4–5 in. deep and use a straight board to make it level. According to the maker's directions, set in any necessary securing bolts at this stage. Once the foundations have hardened, you can begin building up bricks or blocks, using a three to one mixture of sand and cement (measured by bulk). Stick closely to the plans, so that the base wall keeps to the exact greenhouse dimensions. As the walls rise, do not forget to leave spaces for doors and ventilators. Check the vertical truth of the walls frequently using a spirit level and plumb line. If the base wall is very high, or your site slopes slightly, you may need to reinforce it by hammering in sharpened piles.

The final part of the building will depend on your style of greenhouse, but full instructions are usually supplied. Large, modern prefabricated sections should present few difficulties. Popular glazing methods, as already mentioned (p. 12), include sealing strip with non-hardened bitumen and plastic 'strip and clip'. In Dutch light greenhouses, the glass slides into grooves. Always glaze on a dry day if you possibly can.

## Maintenance

Although modern greenhouses need a minimum of attention, there are some chores you cannot avoid. Wooden greenhouses made of hardwoods like oak and teak need little or no treatment to keep them in good condition, though they may well benefit from an occasional oiling with linseed. Red cedar can be left untreated, in which case it will mellow to silver-grey, or it can be treated with a cedar preservative, obtainable from the

Begonias. The greenhouse begonias have huge, opulent blooms and come in a wide range of striking colours and colour combinations.

makers or from garden centres. If pressure-treated in advance, softwoods will last for a long time without painting, though they are not very attractive.

Untreated softwoods will need regular painting to prevent weather damage. Either use white lead paint on top of a priming coat, or, if the wood can be cleaned with a wire brush, apply an aluminium paint, though it is not as attractive or long-lasting as its lead counterpart. If putty has been used for glazing, paint over it and add an eighth to a sixteenth of an inch of paintwork over the glass to give a good seal. Use masking tape to achieve a clean, straight line.

Painting both the outside and the inside of a greenhouse definitely increases the amount of light reflected into it. As an alternative, you can treat wood with a spirit-based preservative, but the job is best done before the house is erected, especially if it is part-plastic. It costs very little to have wood pressure-treated before you buy the greenhouse, and this is even more effective. Alloy and metal houses need no painting, but steel greenhouses may eventually need painting, preferably with aluminium-based paint.

Even if you plan to paint them eventually, treat benches and shelves to begin with, using a spirit-based preservative. Because it gives off damaging fumes, especially when heated, *never* use creosote for this job.

Dirt is the great enemy of the greenhouse gardener. In towns and cities in particular, it sticks to the glass, both inside and out, and cuts down the amount of light passing through the glass. Cleaning the glass does not take very long. For the outside, use a proprietary cleaner or a solution of oxalic acid – one pound to a gallon of water. Spray it on to the glass and wash it off with the hose pipe. To clean the inside, any good detergent will do, but remove the plants before you begin. Use a scraper to get rid of moss and algae growing over the glass and wash them away with a jet of water. Moss is most likely to grow on the north side of a greenhouse and, if prevalent, you may have to replace a few panes of glass occasionally.

Once a year give the inside of the base walls a good scrub and whitewash them. Give the heating pipes an occasional coat of aluminium paint. Contrary to popular belief, this will not impair their heating performance.

## Heating a greenhouse

Heating an ordinary house and heating a greenhouse have much in common, yet it is easy to become confused because of all the talk about the efficiency of different methods. However, the science of heating is a precise science, and it is easy, once you know how, to calculate the cost and efficiency of each method.

Any heating engineer worthy of his name will start an appraisal of a heating project by calculating the heat loss of a building. The first figures to know are those for the heat-moving, and thus the heat-losing powers of various materials. Known as the *thermal conductivities* of substances, these powers are measured in standard British Thermal Units (BTUs) and universally accepted as follows:

|  | Heat conducted per sq. ft. per hour for every degree F. |
| --- | --- |
| Glass (including its framework) | 1.1 BTU per hour |
| 4½ in. brick or composition block | 0.5 BTU per hour |
| Double brick wall, 9 in. thick | 0.4 BTU per hour |
| Wood 1 in. thick | 0.5 BTU per hour |
| Asbestos (sheet or corrugated) | 1.1 BTU per hour |
| Concrete 4 in. thick | 0.75 BTU per hour |
| Double glazed glass (properly sealed) | 0.5 BTU per hour |

This table shows that glass loses heat more than twice as fast as wood or brick, and that double glazing cuts heat loss by half. Technically speaking, heat is also lost through the floor, but this is usually ignored, as the ground area of the greenhouse often stores heat very effectively by throwing it back into the greenhouse.

To calculate the heat loss of your own greenhouse, you must now measure up the total areas of glass and brick, cement or wood in square feet, and multiply each by the above figure for the thermal conductivity. The plan sheets are easiest to use for this.

The heat lost by this perfectly tight greenhouse of our example – a theoretical, rather than a practical figure – is 259 BTUs per hour. But an average greenhouse is bound to have some leaks. A very exposed greenhouse will lose more heat than the norm, a sheltered one less. A realistic addition to the heat loss is a third of the normal, giving here a figure of 343 BTUs.

Having made your calculation, you must now decide how much you want to heat the greenhouse. This will depend, of course, on where you live and what you want to grow. A greenhouse kept at 65 °F in all weather will need a 'lift' of some 45–50 °F over the outside temperature, assuming that this may drop as low as 20 °F. To work out the heat input, simply multiply the heat loss, in this case 343 BTUs by 45 or 50. For a temperate or intermediate house multiply by 35, for a cool

A through-flow type electric greenhouse heater. Such heaters have the advantages of keeping the air in the greenhouse circulating and of ensuring that all parts are heated properly.

house by 20 or 25. As a sample calculation, $343 \times 35$ gives 12,005. This is the number of BTUs needed to heat the intermediate greenhouse, whatever your heat supply.

But these calculations represent the ideal. In practice there are several factors which can influence your heat equation. The most important of these concerns the properties of glass, for while glass is a first-rate transmitter of heat and the heat of the sun passes through it with ease, it is, at the same time, a poor insulator. This means that while glass, unlike plastic, can trap a large spectrum of the sun's heat waves, it cannot store heat for long. Once the temperature outside the greenhouse drops, glass will quickly transmit the heat back again, while plastic, being a good insulator, will retain it.

Reducing the area of glass in your greenhouse will, of course, cut down this heat loss, but a great deal of warmth will be sacrificed unnecessarily if your greenhouse has badly-fitting doors and ventilators, or is poorly glazed. A high wind outside the house will step up the heat loss even further.

Double glazing is effective in reducing wasted heat because it traps a pocket of insulating air between two layers of sealed glass. Although costly, double-glazed greenhouses are on the market, but an alternative, albeit a rather crude one, is to line your greenhouse internally with polythene. If you do this, remember to leave the ventilators free, and bear in mind that

37

you may need to fit extractor fans to cope with the increased condensation.

In Britain's changeable climate, artificial heating is the only way of keeping a greenhouse at a reasonable temperature all the year round. The amount your heating will cost will depend on the fuel you choose, on the sophistication of the system – it could be automatic or semi-automatic to save you work and worry – and the efficiency of the heat-producing units. All systems waste some heat, usually through the flue pipes, but any reputable supplier will give you an accurate estimate of total costs.

There are three main methods of heating a greenhouse:

**Hot pipes.** These contain hot water which is, in turn, heated by a boiler fired by solid fuel, oil, gas or electricity. The simplest boilers will need daily stoking, but some solid-fuel systems are semi-automatic. If you choose a new gas, oil or electric boiler, then it will work on a completely automatic electric-powered time-switch.

**Oil heaters** can either be simple oil stoves which heat the air in the greenhouse direct, or consist of more complicated pressure jet or vaporized burners which heat air in perforated polythene pipes, possibly with the assistance of fans. Electricity is needed to work these fans, and the pressure jet burners, and can be used to control a thermostat system. Unsophisticated oil heaters must be regulated by hand.

**Electrical** heating systems themselves come in five different designs, each ideal for automatic control:

*1. Soil or bench warming cables* heat the growing medium, but have little effect on the air temperature inside the greenhouse.

*2. Mineral insulated cables* are installed round the walls of the greenhouse and held in place by porcelain clips.

*3. Tubular heaters* come in many shapes and sizes and are best fitted to the greenhouse walls.

*4. Fan heaters* can be placed anywhere, but work best in the centre of the house. The largest fan heaters, however, are placed at one end of the greenhouse and hot air is distributed through perforated polythene pipes.

*5. Storage heaters* are useful but some experts discount them because they make the temperature difficult to control.

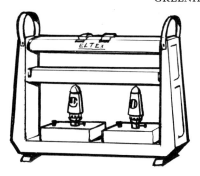 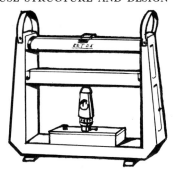

Typical paraffin heaters for greenhouses. Such heaters are safe to use, economical to run and in many instances can be controlled by a thermostat.

Once you have produced a high temperature inside your greenhouse the next problem will be to distribute it evenly, particularly in cold weather. Hot water pipes are the best by far. Transmitting heat by the convection currents of rising hot air, they can set up a warm curtain of air around the greenhouse. And by the process of radiation they warm the soil, a special bonus for heat-loving crops like tomatoes. Benches, too, will benefit from hot water pipes, but the pipes will only work efficiently if kept at the same temperature all along their length. Place the pipes round the edges of the greenhouse.

A heater which merely pumps out warm air from one spot is not ideal, especially in a freezing snap or when one side of the greenhouse is exposed to a prevailing cold wind. These heaters, which work entirely through convection, will be far more useful if they can be fitted to fans or, even better, to a network of perforated polythene pipes to push the air out evenly. But whatever your choice, do not hesitate to seek the advice of a heating expert.

When selecting pipes to carry hot water, decide on the modern $1\frac{1}{4}$-in. diameter, rather than the old 4-in. system. Although you will need a greater length of the small-bore pipe, and it will cool down quickly, it will save you money because there is much less water to heat. In addition, the narrow pipes will give you much better control over the greenhouse temperature, as they respond quickly to the demands of the thermostat.

If you plan to install a very large footage of $1\frac{1}{4}$-in. pipe, there may be some problems when it comes to water circulation, so budget for a circulating pump. If the difference in temperature between the water in the pipes and the air in the greenhouse is 100 °F, the amount of heat given off by them, per foot, will be:

| TYPE OF SYSTEM | AVERAGE OPERATIONAL EFFICIENCY | APPROX. RUNNING COSTS PER 100,000 B.T.U s. (Therm) at fuel prices as stated. | |
|---|---|---|---|
| Solid fuel boiler, simple design. Hard coal. | 50% | Based on coal at 125,000 BTU per cwt. Cost of fuel per cwt. | 75p = 9½p per therm<br>70p = 9p per therm<br>65p = 8½p per therm<br>60p = 7½p per therm |
| More refined solid fuel boiler using smokeless fuel or coke | 60% | Based on a value of 12,000 BTU/lb. Cost of fuel per cwt. | 75p = 9½p per therm<br>70p = 9p per therm<br>65p = 8p per therm |
| | 70% | | 75p = 8p per therm<br>70p = 7½p per therm<br>65p = 7p per therm |
| Purpose-made oil-fired boiler and fan heaters with external flue (some types have no flue and this results in slightly higher operational efficiency) | 75% | Based on oil at 162,000 BTU per gallon. Cost of fuel per gall. (Bulk buy. Small quantities may be up to 25% more.) | 7½p = 6½p per therm<br>7p = 6p per therm<br>6½p = 5½p per therm<br>6p = 5p per therm |
| Converted oil-fired boiler with vaporizer type burner (Figures for free-standing oil heaters are fairly similar but are generally more advantageous in respect of running costs only) | 70% | Based on oil at 158,000 BTU per gallon. Cost of fuel per gall. bulk buy. | 8p = 7p per therm<br>7½p = 6½p per therm<br>7p = 6p per therm<br>6½p = 5½p per therm |
| Purpose-made gas-fired boiler | 75–80% | Base the cost on price of gas per therm, which varies from area to area, but deduct 20–25% for loss of efficiency | |
| All types of electrical heaters (Residual heat from storage heaters is considerable and is difficult to allow for in comparative tables. Off-peak tariffs are usually lower than those stated here, but cannot be considered for) | 100% | Based on normal tariff— Cost per unit* | 1p = 24p per therm<br>0.54p = 16p per therm<br>0.52p = 15p per therm<br>0.5p = 14½p per therm<br>0.47p = 14p per therm<br>0.45p = 13½p per therm |

\* Allow for primary unit costs.

| DIAMETER | HEAT EMITTED (to nearest round figures) |
|----------|------------------------------------------|
| 1 in. | 80 BTU |
| $1\frac{1}{4}$ in. | 100 BTU |
| $1\frac{1}{2}$ in. | 110 BTU |
| 2 in. | 130 BTU |
| $2\frac{1}{2}$ in. | 150 BTU |
| 3 in. | 190 BTU |
| $3\frac{1}{2}$ in. | 200 BTU |
| 4 in. | 230 BTU |

To work out how much piping you will need, divide the figure above into the total heat load for the greenhouse which you worked out before.

Armed with all the economic arguments about various heating systems, you can now go ahead and choose the one which suits you best for price and convenience. On the whole, pipe systems, whatever the heating method, are most economical to run, but much depends on the cost of the fuel, and they are more expensive to install. The cheapest sort of oil burner – rather than oil stove – is a vaporizing one, which is installed in a steel or cast-iron jacket. Rely on expert installation if you choose this system. Unless the flame and the draught are carefully regulated, much of the gas produced will be wasted.

Always put the boiler on the side of the greenhouse which is sheltered from the prevailing winds. This will stop flue gases from staining the glass. If you can, put the boiler outside the house, on the north side – it will work more efficiently, be protected from the wind and emit a steadier draught.

The advice of a heating engineer or horticulturalist is a must before installing a pipe system. The final layout will depend on the pipe diameter you choose and on whether you add a pump to assist the circulation. In general, pipes work best on the so-called *thermo-syphon principle*. The pipes rise one inch in every ten feet, and at the highest point in the system there is a tank or valve. The temperature in the pipes is kept constant because hot water rises, is cooled and falls to the bottom of the system. A drainage point – fixed on the boiler or return pipe – is vital. From it, the pipes can be drained when not in use during cold weather, to prevent cracking, a procedure which is *all important*.

Tubular heaters are one of the most reliable and economic ways of heating a greenhouse. *Courtesy of Humex.*

Modern circulating pumps largely do away with the need for a thermo-syphon system, which means that pipe layouts can be much more flexible. Pipes can be put where they fit most conveniently, and flexible rubber couplings can be used instead of metal ones. They can be used under benches for propagation, then dropped to ground level when the benches are removed to plant, for example, a crop of tomatoes. This particular versatility is especially useful for providing heat for warmth-loving crops.

Control is simplicity itself if you have an electrically-operated system, for it can be linked up to a thermostat which gives a high degree of control. Constant attention, however, is the only secret of success with a simple oil-fired stove. Solid-fuel boilers, too, need much care if they are to keep the greenhouse temperature even, but today's gas and oil pipe systems are self-regulating from a thermostat within the greenhouse. Any pipe system which is thermo-syphoned, however, whether heated by solid fuel or by oil, will be demanding on effort, but these can be made easier to control if fitted, respectively, with a thermostatic flue regulator or a thermostatic control which automatically lights or extinguishes the flame. A pipe system which depends exclusively on a circulating pump can be

An aluminium lean-to greenhouse with direct access to the dwelling house. Such greenhouses are easily heated from the domestic heating system.

controlled through a thermostat linked to the pump itself, rather than to the boiler. This means that the boiler can be left to reach its own temperature and is constantly poised to supply heat, but is dangerous if pipes are made of cast iron, for these may be damaged by sudden expansion. An electrically-operated valve will have much the same sort of controlling effect.

In a porch or conservatory, it is tempting to install off-peak storage heaters which run off the domestic supply, but these may not be very efficient. A simple on/off heater will, for example, produce too much heat on a warm day following a cold night. Even with a storage heater which has a controllable input and output you may need to fit proper ventilators to regulate the temperature effectively. Another alternative is to heat your porch or conservatory with narrow hot water pipes from the household supply, but control will again be a problem if your time-switch is set to halt the heater overnight. Better still, keep the boiler temperature constant. Link one time control clock to the circulating pump of the domestic supply and fit a separate pump to the conservatory system. If the conservatory system is self-contained, it can be regulated with temperature-sensitive valves within the pipes. Hot air heating will present you with very similar problems, so always take the trouble to seek expert help.

## Ventilation and shading

Controlling the heat of a greenhouse is closely linked with other environmental problems, especially those of ventilation and shade. Because warm air is lighter than cold air, it rises, and if this air escapes through ventilators, then heat, and also humidity, can be controlled with ease. The best place for vents is usually – though not inevitably – the highest point of the greenhouse. As the hot air escapes, cold air is drawn in through the vents, either by simple exchange or under the pressure of the wind. It comes in, too, through glass overlaps, gaps under the door and any other poor fittings.

The rate at which air change takes place depends mainly on the size and position of the ventilators. Ventilators placed low down, through which cool air will rush in, can speed up the air

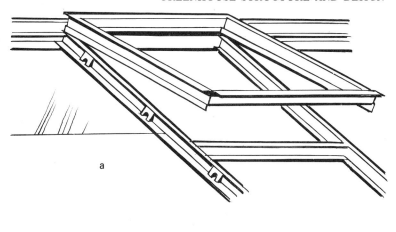

a

Two different types of ventilator.
(a) is the fan-light type, and (b) the louvre type.

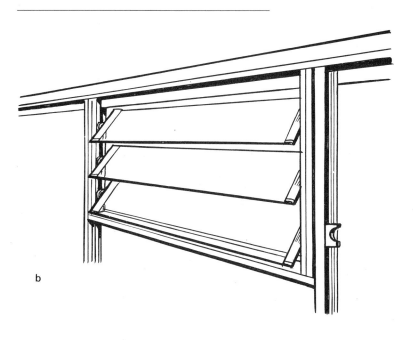

b

change enormously. Fit ones of louvre design which you can open or close at your own discretion, and if possible make sure that the total area of ventilator is at least a fifth of the floor area, calculated with the vents wide open, though, in fact, many small greenhouses are poorly supplied with ventilation, and you may have to settle for less than the perfect situation.

Extractor fans are first rate for greenhouse ventilation, with the proviso that they change the air 50–60 times per hour and that they do not create high wind speeds which could damage plants or slow their growth. The best fans, therefore, are large ones, with slow rotations and overlapped so that air will not enter when the fan is not working. Make sure that there is a good air inlet opposite the fan. For even greater control, you can fit the fan with a time-switch.

The latest method of ventilating a greenhouse is that of air-conditioning. Cool, outside air is pushed into the house and escapes through leaks in its superstructure, through plastic vents which open when the air pressure reaches a certain level. When the humidity drops, the air is moistened by an automatically-controlled humidifier, and heaters may also be linked into the system. A time clock is useful for adapting the fans to turn off and on at intervals throughout summer nights and thus prevent an excessive build-up of condensation.

Conventional ventilators are easily adapted to fit into an air-conditioning system. Electrical attachments will ensure that the vents open when the greenhouse reaches a certain temperature, by pulling them unshut on a cable or by operating a 'winder'. Less expensive are ventilator 'lifts' which react to rises in temperature by expanding and lifting clear of the ventilator, thus letting cold air in. So apart from a few ventilators which you would open by hand in very hot weather, your entire greenhouse air-conditioning can be remote controlled.

For many pot plants, for successful early propagation and for treating tomatoes suffering from attack by *Verticillium* wilt, the best way of cutting down the heat in the greenhouse is by

Grapes are always considered one of the most exotic delicacies that can be grown ▶
in the greenhouse. If properly trained very heavy crops can be obtained for relatively little effort.

*Left* A Propagating Unit control. This is easily adjusted by removing the small rubber protective cap and turning the dial with a screw-driver. *Courtesy of Humex.* *Right* A simple greenhouse thermostat heating control unit. A unit of this type is relatively inexpensive. *Courtesy of Humex.*

shading. Blinds – either the venetian or roller kind – are effective, particularly if green in colour, and can be fixed either inside or outside the greenhouse. Although it gives you less flexibility, painting the outside of the glass with a mixture of lime and water, plus a little size, is equally effective, as the whiteness reflects, rather than absorbs sunlight. Or you can buy a branded green coloured shading, but both will wash off over the summer months and any colouring still in place in October can be brushed off so that plants get as much light as possible during the winter months.

# 2 Basic Equipment

## Benches and shelves – watering – soil warming – propagation units – lighting

### Benches and shelves

Benches and shelves are a useful addition to any greenhouse, and planned with imagination will give you not only storage space but also much more room for all sorts of activities. Slatted benches, made of lengths of pressure-treated wood measuring 4 in. $\times \frac{3}{4}$ in., and fitted into iron or galvanized steel fitments, are ideal for housing pot plants, boxes of seedlings and for propagation done in boxes or pots, for warm air will filter easily between the slats. Solid benches made of wood, galvanized corrugated iron or asbestos are best filled with rooting mediums for raising cuttings or used for mist propagation (see p. 54). Like slatted benches, they are best constructed at table height – 30–34 in. – and made 3–3$\frac{1}{2}$ ft. wide.

Some gardeners think that solid benches should be used exclusively for pot plants, and there is some sense in this argument, but whatever you decide on, always make sure that there is an air space between the bench and the greenhouse wall so that hot air can percolate upwards.

Shelves, fixed high up, are very useful for keeping plants near the light during the winter months. Or you can have two tiers of benches. Use the upper tier for propagation, seedlings

Propagating Unit controls. The temperature in the sand can be checked by withdrawing the special thermometer. *Courtesy of Humex.*

The inside of a propagating case showing the air-warming cables attached round the side of the case. *Courtesy of Humex.*

and so on, the lower tier for storing dahlia tubers or chrysanthemum stools over the winter.

# Watering

Your greenhouse watering equipment need amount to nothing more than a watering can and a cold water tap, but you may want to follow the lead of commercial greenhouse gardeners and install an automatic or semi-automatic watering system. Water is sprayed on to plants from above or at soil level, or reaches pot plants through individual tubes. Controlled electronically, the water can have soluble nutrients added, though in this case the system has to have a dilutor fitted. A dilutor is simply a bottle of water fitted between the tap and the hose outlet which literally 'waters down' the chemicals.

Rather than fitting a completely automatic system, many amateur gardeners prefer to water their greenhouses with a fine mist from a special pipe called a sprayline. These spraylines are easy to fit into a small greenhouse, and will work well as long as the pressure and volume of the water is high enough. Electrically-operated valves can be attached to the system, and these inexpensive devices mean that you can direct water on to your plants at the flick of a switch.

Ceramic blocks can be fitted into the greenhouse water supply. These control the amount of water being released, as water rapidly evaporates from their porous surfaces. When choosing watering cans for the house, select those with long spouts and fine roses, in either metal or plastic.

The Humex 'Tricklematic' fully-automatic watering system. Such systems are, in fact, a far more reliable way of supplying plants regularly with the right amount of water than haphazard can-watering. *Courtesy of Humex.*

If you decide to specialize in growing pot plants, it might be well worth considering a capillary watering system, though you can use one for other growing projects too. In principle, a completely level solid bench is lined with polythene to make a completely watertight basin 3 or 4 in. deep, and a perforated pipe placed to run down the centre of the bench. The basin is then filled with rough, gritty sand which will draw up the water.

51

The pipe for the capillary bench is best placed inside some drainage tiles or sections of curved asbestos, as this will help prevent the holes in the pipe from getting blocked. By attaching the bottom end of the pipe to a fish tank fitted with a ball cock it is easy to keep a steady water level between $\frac{1}{2}$ in. and 1 in. below the surface of the sand. Or you can operate a capillary set-up with a slow-running hose or possibly special drip nozzles which, as their name suggests, drip water constantly on to the sand. For the greatest possible sophistication, the water input can be electronically controlled.

Placed on top of the sand in the bench, pot plants will absorb water by capillary action – the sucking power is produced by the plant roots and by the water-attracting properties of the sand. As long as you do not make them too strong, solutions of mineral nutrients can be added to the bench. Choose plastic rather than clay pots. They will work more efficiently. Once constructed, a capillary bench like this is easy to adapt for growing tomatoes by the 'ring culture' method (see p. 107) and for other crops.

# Soil warming

The soil in your greenhouse borders or benches can be adapted to grow heat-loving plants simply by warming it, or you can get good results by warming the benches or pots themselves. Provided the growing medium is warm, many plants will grow well in cool air. This means that the growing medium – soil, bench or pot – can be kept warm very cheaply, and that there is no need to heat the whole greenhouse. The warming process is particularly effective if used *before* planting tomatoes or other plants that thrive on heat. For while the soil quickly heats up if warmed directly, the same process takes a long time, and is much more costly, if only the air in the greenhouse is warmed by pipes which do not touch the growing substrata. Another advantage of soil warming is in the field of propagation. Often, you will want to heat a small amount of soil or compost to a high temperature, in order to assist rapid rooting. If so, a soil-warming system will prove invaluable.

The method of soil warming is quite uncomplicated: electric cable of 12-gauge wire is laid 9 or 10 in. deep and 3–9 in. apart. The wire is then connected to a series of transformers which act to keep the voltage down to between 6 and 30 volts, the ideal for safety. The total wattage of the circuit (the voltage multiplied by the amps or current running through the wire) should lie somewhere between 5 and 10 watts per sq. ft. Twelve-gauge wire is first rate for warming borders and cold frames, and benches can be heated either on this system or direct from the mains. The mains are the best source of electricity if you are attempting mist propagation, for the extra power makes it possible to keep the temperature at the perfect value of 75 °F. In this case, the wattage will be about 15 watts per sq. ft.

There are three ways of controlling your soil-warming equipment. The most popular is the dosage method, in which the heating element is turned on for a fixed period every day or every night, when electricity is obtainable at a cheap, off-peak rate. The temperature of the soil will fall very little while the heating is turned off. Although 8 or 10 hours of heating in every 24 will probably be enough, you can link the system to a time-switch.

The second heating method is via a thermostat embedded horizontally in the soil. Not necessary for most amateur operations, this control system is particularly well suited to growing plants which constantly demand high temperatures. Thirdly, you can simply insert a thermometer into the soil and turn the electricity on or off as you think fit. But if in doubt, you can be sure of good advice from your local electricity board, from a qualified electrician or from equipment suppliers.

## Propagation units

Success in propagation will depend almost entirely on your ability to persuade cuttings of stems or leaves to make roots, and thus become self-supporting, as quickly as possible. The greatest problem is to keep the stem healthy all the while, for viable roots are unlikely to form if, above ground, soft leaf tissue is in the process of wilting. But in a propagation case, the temperature and humidity of the air are higher than normal. The loss of moisture from the leaves – a process called transpiration – is thus cut down to a minimum. The tissues of stem and leaf stay full of water, and stiff, making propagation much easier, root formation more rapid.

 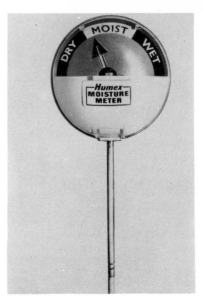

The 'tank' of a capillary watering system. Such systems do away with the need for regular hand-watering. *Courtesy of Humex.*

A moisture meter. Such meters are the most accurate method yet devised of deciding when a plant needs watering. *Courtesy of Humex.*

The most humble sort of propagating case is a polythene bag. Placed over a box or pot it will efficiently retain both heat and moisture. A sheet of glass over a box will have the same effect. More complex propagating cases consist of a solid bench, which can be filled with the growing medium, and which is heated, covered by a 'frame' made of glass or polythene. In addition, the case can be fully lit, and the whole carefully controlled by means of a thermostat, quite independently of the temperature and humidity of the greenhouse itself.

One disadvantage of propagating cases is that they may get too hot and, in turn, damage the plants. To avoid this, you could consider installing a mist propagation unit, which heats the soil to a constant temperature of 70–75 °F while, at the same time, spraying the cuttings with a fine mist of water from spray nozzles.

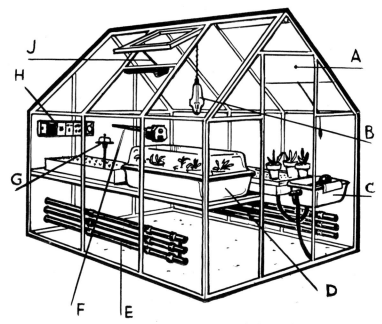

The fully automated greenhouse: all you have to do is watch the plants grow. A Shading blinds on spring rollers: these can be controlled by a photo-electric cell. B An electric fumigator. C Header tank for automatic capillary-action watering system. D Propagator case with earth cable heating wires, and automatic temperature control. E Automatic tubular heaters controlled by, F rod-type thermostat. G Mist propagation unit. H Control panel. J Automatically operated ventilator.

## Lighting

Although you may want to light your greenhouse to change the length of the day or intensify the radiance of the sun in spring or autumn, the main use of lighting is to make working in the greenhouse possible in winter and during the evenings. Make sure that you fix the lights in positions which do not cast too much shadow and where you do not have to constantly duck to avoid them. This will throw light out to best advantage all over the greenhouse. And you can add extra bulbs to light benches or dark corners which you use frequently in winter. Do choose waterproof light fittings.

# 3 Caring for Greenhouse Plants

### The greenhouse environment – plant nutrients
### Basic ingredients – John Innes composts – U/C composts – compost mixing

Knowing something about the way plants live and grow will help you become an expert in your greenhouse. A good mother appreciates the needs of her baby and, in the same way, a good gardener knows just what will make the plants in his care thrive. All green plants have roots, stems and leaves and most bear flowers which mature into fruits containing seeds.

## The greenhouse environment

Because a greenhouse can overcome the changeability of the weather, it will not only support exotic blooms in their natural state but also plants which the breeder has tailored to fruit or flower at times convenient to Man. Although not entirely successful, plant breeding has resulted in a vast range of plants in which the best qualities of different groups and varieties are blended to give the best of quality, colour, disease resistance, fruit production and so on.

The really important thing about a greenhouse is that although it supports plants whose growth cycle is essentially similar from seed or cutting to mature plant, these plants are often far from their natural homes and habitats and so need special care. Tropical plants are not, for example, merely tender and sensitive to frost. Tomatoes, whose original home was sunny South America, yearn, despite intense breeding, for all the light they can get, especially in their early days when we try to persuade them to grow in our dreary winter. Plants from the world's tropical forests crave for the hot, humid, shady environment typical of their home. And a lot of perfectly hardy plants find their way into the greenhouse because there they will grow at an unusual season of the year. Lettuce, for example, is supremely successful out-of-doors in summer, but will thrive during the winter in a heated greenhouse.

The artificial conditions of the greenhouse call for thoroughness and patience when growing plants. Inside the house there is light and air but no moisture unless you supply it. The sun shines in summer, and there is an excessive build-up of heat which has to be remedied. In winter, when there is no sunshine, you have to produce a substitute. In these warm, often humid conditions, plants grow much more quickly, and so need more water and more food than those growing outside.

Another important side-effect of the greenhouse's man-made atmosphere is that there is a tremendous difference between the conditions within during day and night. This is especially so in spring and autumn when warm, sunny days are often followed by cold nights. The result is a huge temperature variation which can result in unbalanced growth.

One of the great advantages of the greenhouse over the great outside is that whereas out-of-doors the results of your efforts will be, after a few years, quite unpredictable, in the greenhouse you can control and predict plant behaviour with considerable accuracy. To get the most out of your greenhouse, take advantage of these special features. Compared with the garden, you can start with the soil or compost which is free from pests and diseases, and whose physical properties are precisely what you want them to be. You start with no weeds, none will arrive unless you introduce them, and you can add or subtract heat, light, nutrients, at will. Because you have such power, use it carefully and do not take chances with doubtful seeds or soil, composts or cuttings. The same factors of total environmental control which enable the plants to grow in the greenhouse to thrive, will also enable weeds, pests and diseases to flourish once they get a hold.

Palm trees come mainly from the tropical and sub-tropical regions of the world. There are a large number of different palms suitable for the cold, cool or heated greenhouse.

The first essentials for plant growth are, as we have seen, light, air and water, plus heat, either to trigger growth or to induce a cutting to produce roots. The demand for these front-line supplies increases as the plant grows. How much it rises is governed to a large extent by how large the plant becomes, by the weather and by the time of year. But plants also need minerals, which are mostly absorbed from the soil via the roots and transported, within the plant, to the sites of growth, flower or fruit production. To help the greenhouse gardener balance up the mineral needs of the plants in his care, fertilizers, liquid feeds and composts are available in vast numbers. But it is as well to know something about what they contain and what the plant will need before you go ahead with any dosage, either to the soil or direct to leaves and stems, for plants can absorb nutrients from these parts as well as from the roots.

## Plant nutrients

No two plants will thrive on exactly the same diet, nor will a seedling necessarily need the same diet as it will when a mature plant. What is most important is a proper *balance* of nutrients, for just as the human frame needs proteins, carbohydrates, fats and vitamins, but in varying amounts, so plants need a mixture of minerals such as nitrogen, potassium and phosphorus.

Another reason for keeping a constant check on the balance of plant nutrients is that plants grow more quickly in the greenhouse than they do out-of-doors. Their requirements therefore change more rapidly. Make sure, then, that the plant nutrients are well maintained throughout the growing period and, if necessary, renew the soil or compost should it have become physically exhausted.

The sort of plants which will grow well in any soil depends to a large extent on the acidity or alkalinity of the soil. The substance which has the greatest effect on this important quality is lime. In chemical terms, lime is made up of the substance calcium carbonate, which is an alkali. Plants need lime, and the calcium carbonate also helps to keep the soil sweet by neutralizing the acids manufactured by micro-organisms.

Chemists record acidity or alkalinity as a number known as the pH value. A lime-rich soil will have a pH of about 8, an acid-rich soil like peat a pH of around 4. The ideal pH for the greenhouse varies from plant to plant, but many will thrive in pure peat or a mixture of peat and sand. But unlike the peat of natural bogland, greenhouse peat preparations contain few micro-organisms so that little acid is produced and the environment remains stable.

Four chemical elements are essential for the health of all plants:

**Nitrogen.** Plants absorb nitrogen from the soil in the form of chemical compounds called nitrates. Nitrogen is needed for

59

the development of the leaves, and probably for all plant growth. But any plant will suffer if you give it either too much or too little nitrogen. An excess of nitrogen, particularly an excess in relation to the amount of potassium the plant is getting, will lead to large fleshy leaves, small flowers and fruits. When nitrogen is in short supply the reverse happens. The leaves are small, flowers and fruits of normal size. The colour of the leaves is a good guide to the amount of nitrogen being supplied. Pale green or yellow means too little, a very dark green too much.

**Potassium.** The role of potassium in the life of plants is a complex one. It is involved in photosynthesis, the process by which, with the help of the green pigment, chlorophyll, in their leaves, plants trap carbon dioxide and combine it with water to make carbohydrates. Potassium is vital to the formation of fruits and seeds and to the manufacture of chlorophyll itself. Give plants potassium in the form of potash – chemically potassium oxide – or as other compounds such as potassium carbonate. The leaves will give you the clues to dosage. Too much potassium results in hard, dark leaves, too little in flabby, pale-green growth. Experience will give you the best guide, but remember that many crops, especially tomatoes, absorb nitrogen and potassium together. Give too much of one, and the plant will not be able to take in the other, so take the trouble to balance each one carefully.

**Phosphorus.** Found in the soil in chemical combinations called phosphates, phosphorus is essential to plants because it is involved in the growth and development of roots, stems, leaves and flowers. Without phosphorus, plants cannot use the carbohydrates they build up in photosynthesis, and cannot manufacture new cells. Good root production and early maturity are both impossible without phosphorus, but an excess or deficiency of this element is very difficult to pinpoint just by looking at a plant. The best guide to a phosphorus shortage, however, is a dark-green or bluish tinge on the leaves.

**Magnesium.** Underrated in importance until recent years, magnesium, like potassium is involved in the vital process of photosynthesis. Some crops, including tomatoes, have large demands for magnesium but the element is absorbed alongside potassium, and both elements are needed for proper magnesium uptake. Most soils have plenty of natural magnesium, but a plant suffering from a lack of it will have pale leaves which later turn bronze. Too much magnesium is a rare problem and unlikely to cause you trouble.

## The basic ingredients of composts

Good feeding in the greenhouse will be enhanced if you put plant roots in high-quality soil or some other growing medium. While ordinary garden soil may be enriched with compost or 'humus' formed from the breakdown of grass cuttings and other garden refuse, professional gardeners usually use the word compost to mean specially-prepared mixtures, enriched with nutrients, which form an excellent environment for the roots of greenhouse plants.

Composts are mixtures of various substances, of which the most important are as follows:

**Loam.** Ideally, loam is the end-product of the partial rotting of turf from a grass pasture 4–5 in. thick stacked grass-downwards for about 6 months. Depending on the soil and the quality of the grass, loam can vary enormously. Really reliable loam is, in fact, difficult to come by, but a good substitute is the top 9–12 in. of the soil, though this will be low in organic matter and variable in mineral supply. If using this 'second best' loam, always avoid soil which you know has been infested with diseases and pests like potato root eelworm and choose material whose particles are neither too coarse, like sand or too fine like clay. Check the acidity of the loam and sterilize it.

**Peat.** If he lives in Britain, a greenhouse gardener can choose from many different kinds of peat, but the ideal peat for composts is light in colour and open in texture. Avoid dark, fine 'dirty' peats, or those with a black, decomposed look, or use them sparingly with cellular peat to step up its mineral content. If in doubt, wet the peat and press out the water. The darker it is, the less desirable the peat.

In compost, good-quality peat acts like a sponge and so helps the growing medium to store both water and vital nutrients. And at the same time it allows air to get to the plant roots. A high-quality peat, supplied in a polythene bag to keep it moist, can be guaranteed to be free of pests and disease-carrying micro-organisms. Peat is most valuable to plants in

61

This flourishing array of plants is being grown on a gravel tray watered by a capilliary watering system. Water trickles through the gravel, and the plants take up just sufficient water for their needs. *Courtesy of Humex.*

the long, rather than the short, term. The minerals it contains cannot be used immediately, but over a matter of months peat encourages growth of micro-organisms which, in turn make the nutrients absorbable.

**Leaf mould.** Once used very widely in compost-making, leaf mould has recently fallen from favour because its quality is too variable. Despite this, you can make good use of a well-matured leaf mould from a mixed deciduous wood. Compost containing leaf mould is particularly good for growing tomatoes and chrysanthemums which demand nourishment over a long period.

**Sand.** Whatever its 'grain grading', small amounts of sand will give a compost body and porosity. Always select sand that is neither acid nor alkaline. Make sure that it is free from

Zinnias like these colourful 'California Giants' are amongst the gayest of annuals, and excellent for cutting. Seed needs to be sown in the greenhouse.

contamination and, for preference, intermediate in texture.

**Vermiculite or Perlite.** These two substances, made respectively of expanded mica and of volcanic ash, are valuable additions to compost as they can absorb large amounts of water. Although their names may be unfamiliar, neither is a newcomer to the horticultural scene, and they can be bought from reputable suppliers.

## The John Innes composts

Extremely useful in the greenhouse, John Innes composts were first compounded, and their ingredients standardized by W. J. C. Lawrence and W. J. Newall of the John Innes Horticultural Institution. Although available ready mixed, you can make up your own compost to the basic John Innes formula.

**John Innes seed compost**, for both seeds and very young plants, is especially useful in winter. Its ingredients are:

two parts (by bulk) of loam, preferably sterilized by heat
one part (by bulk) of peat
one part (by bulk) of coarse sand

To every bushel of the mixture – a cube measuring $22 \times 10 \times 12$ in. – add $\frac{3}{4}$ oz. ground limestone and $1\frac{1}{2}$ oz. superphosphate.

**John Innes potting compost** has the following composition:

seven parts (by bulk) of loam
three parts (by bulk) of peat
two parts (by bulk) of coarse sand

To this basic mixture, other materials are added, in varying amounts, and each resulting compost dubbed with a number. The No. 1 compost is enriched with $\frac{3}{4}$ oz. ground limestone, and $\frac{1}{4}$ lb. John Innes base fertilizer (which is two parts by weight of hoof and horn meal, two parts superphosphates of lime and one part sulphate of potash) in every bushel. For the No. 2 compost, add $\frac{1}{2}$ lb. of the base fertilizer. For the No. 3 compost, add $\frac{3}{4}$ lb. of the base fertilizer.

Each John Innes compost is suited to a particular job in the greenhouse. Choose potting compost No. 1 for young, newly pricked-off seedlings. As long as the seedlings are housed in large enough pots, the compost will contain enough nutrients to feed the plants until they are ready for repotting. Do not transplant these seedlings directly into potting compost No. 2. Instead, use John Innes No. 1 but add liquid feed as soon as they start to grow vigorously, particularly if the weather is dull, the temperature low.

The No. 2 compost is ideal for adding to a growing medium which is supporting ring cultures of tomatoes or other plants which have a long growing season. Reserve the No. 3 compost for more mature plants, such as chrysanthemums, which will not be damaged by its high fertilizer content.

# The U/C composts

Work carried out at the University of California has given the greenhouse gardener another range of composts. There are

In this greenhouse advantage has been taken of the greenhouse border, of intermediate staging and high-level staging. Ferns or ground cover plants could also be grown under the staging on the right.

a great number of different formulae, but all are based on a peat composed of moss sphagnum plus fine sand. To these, various nutrients are added. You can either buy U/C composts already made up, or you can buy the basic substance plus fertilizer to add as you require, but it is worth remembering that U/C composts have very few mineral reserves and that you will have to administer constant feeds of liquid nutrients from early on. Yet these composts are very useful because they are sterile, that is, free from pests and harmful micro-organisms. There are several popular U/C mixes:

**For winter and early spring.** Use equal parts, by bulk, of peat moss and fine sand and add to each bushel (a quantity $22 \times 12 \times 10$ in.)

$\frac{1}{5}$ oz. nitrate of potash     6 oz. magnesium limestone
$\frac{1}{5}$ oz. sulphate of potash     2 oz. ground limestone
2 oz. superphosphates

**For spring and summer.** Use equal amounts, by bulk, of peat moss and sand. Add to each bushel of the mixture:

65

Impatiens or 'Busy Lizzy', a greenhouse plant that flowers for about nine months of the year. There are forms with red, pink or purple flowers, also with striped flowers or variegated leaves.

| | |
|---|---|
| 4 oz. hoof and horn meal | 2 oz. superphosphates |
| $\frac{1}{4}$ oz. ammonium nitrate | 4 oz. ground limestone |
| 1 oz. sulphate of potash | 2 oz. magnesium limestone |

One word of warning. *Never* add the hoof and horn meal until just before you use the compost. Care should be taken not to overwater the U/C composts.

Experience will tell you which recipes work best, but some gardeners prefer to add between 5 and 8 oz. of ground limestone to the spring and summer compost, plus a slow-acting fertilizer containing traces of the minerals iron and manganese. Others prefer a mix of 75 per cent peat and 25 per cent sand, yet others the exact reverse of this. A coarse sand may give better results, and is certainly more popular, than a fine one.

**For full season growing**, U/C composts can be used in

Gloxinias. In spite of their exotic appearance gloxinias are easy to grow in the greenhouse. The ones shown here have double flowers.

containers, but the plants will suffer unless they are constantly fed.

## Compost mixing

Always keep your compost ingredients under cover and make sure that they are reasonably dry. The best place for mixing is a cement floor. First put down the most bulky ingredient (usually loam) followed by peat and sand. Turn the total several times before finally adding the fertilizers, carefully measured. Add each one individually, and mix well each time. *Before you use the compost, leave it to warm up in the greenhouse.*

# 4 Pot Plants

## Pot plant needs – flowering plants – ferns

Though still far from rivalling the Dutch in the number and excellence of their pot plants, Britain's greenhouse gardeners are fast realizing the pleasures of cultivating these members of the indoor team. With a little persistence plus plenty of common sense you can produce a whole galaxy of colour and variety. Your greenhouse will not only provide you with the absorbing interest of pot plants, but will mean plants in your home all the year round.

## Pot plant needs

Pot plants vary enormously in their habits and grow and flower at different times throughout the year. The secret of success is knowing when the plants need water and nutrients, controlling the environment carefully, selecting the right compost and putting it in a pot which is neither too big nor too small. Except for cacti and slow-growing pot plants like ferns, most actively-growing pot plants will need a liquid feed every 10–14 days. Although you may be far from 100 per cent successful, especially at the start, do persevere with pot plants in the greenhouse. With experience, you will find them a most rewarding hobby.

As far as equipment is concerned, what you need for growing

68

pot plants is a well-situated, properly-ventilated greenhouse free from drips. It should have a good clean water supply and a heating system which can keep the temperature at about 50–55 °F. Inside the greenhouse you will need a fairly extensive layout of benches. A tiered set-up will not only create more space, but will make your display look more attractive. Keep a convenient corner of a bench, either in the greenhouse or in a near-by shed, for potting up plants. You may also get good use from a storage area to house compost ingredients, though this is far from essential now that reliably-formulated mixtures can be easily obtained. Make sure you have enough room for storing pots and seedboxes and bear in mind the possibility of fixing a permanent propagating case, though you can easily make do with a temporary 'rooting bench' for a few years.

The way you start off your pot plants will depend on the individual species. Some are perfectly successful started from seed while others are best propagated from cuttings, which you may have to beg from friends or neighbours, either as cuttings themselves or in the form of stock plants. Plan your planting carefully so that each plant is in the right place at the right time of year, and be sure to use the correct compost.

# Flowering plants

The range of pot plants which will thrive in a frost-free greenhouse is enormous, but keep to a few simple sorts to begin with. Primulas, pelargoniums, coleuses, fuchsias and many annuals make excellent pot plants and are relatively simple to grow. Many cacti are simplicity itself, but tuberous begonias, cinerarias or streptocarpus can be a little more difficult.

**Annuals in pots.** Some of the best annuals to grow in pots inside the greenhouse, to give both colour and cut flowers are:

| | |
|---|---|
| Acroclinium | Larkspur |
| Antirrhinum (technically a perennial) | Nasturtium |
| Arctotis | Nemesia |
| Calendula | Petunia |
| Felicia | Ursinia |
| Godetia | Zinnia |

Sow the seeds in March or April and pot out the seedlings in 3-in. pots. Then simply supply them with moderate heat.

69

**Orchids.** At present there is much interest in orchid-growing, but it need not be the exclusive province of the professional. Many orchids merely need a frost-free greenhouse rather than stove heat, but all demand humidity and shade in summer. The basic compost for orchid-growing is equal parts of sphagnum moss and fibre from the fern osmunda. Add some broken crocks to give good drainage. Rather than risking disappointment, it is well worth taking the time to consult a book devoted to orchid-growing, and you can also join one of the Orchid Societies.

None of the following orchids is difficult.

# For the Cool Greenhouse

| | |
|---|---|
| Cymbidium | Oncidium |
| Paphiopedilum (some) | Coelogyne |
| Odontoglossum | Dendrobium |

# For the Warm Greenhouse

| | |
|---|---|
| Cattleya | × Laeliocattleya |
| × Brassolaeliocattleya | Paphiopedilums |

# For the Stove House

| | |
|---|---|
| Phalaenopsis | Vanda |

**Alpines.** A cool greenhouse is an excellent place to grow alpine plants. These natives of the world's mountain ranges will make your greenhouse both colourful and interesting. Like orchid-growing, this is rather specialized, and you will gain much from becoming a member of an Alpine Society or Rock Garden Club.

# Alpines

Andromeda, *Campanula garganica*, Cassiope, Crocus (winter flowering), Cyclamen, Cytisus, Dianthus, Dodecatheon, Draba, *Dryas octopetala*, Dwarf conifers, Hepatica, Helleborus, Lewisia, Narcissus (dwarf types), Primula, Rhodohypoxis, Saxifraga, Sedum, Sempervivum.

As well as specific pot plants, many shrubs and herbaceous plants will bloom much earlier in the year if potted and cultivated in the greenhouse. The list of plants is virtually endless.

African violets are easily raised from leaf-cuttings in a propagating case in the greenhouse. One of the best mediums for growing established plants is shredded newspaper.

**Wall plants and shrubs.** Many tender wall plants and shrubs are ideal occupants for a lean-to greenhouse. Choose, for a start, from any of these:

| | |
|---|---|
| *Cobaea scandens* | *Jasminum* |
| *Ipomoea rubro-caerulea* | *Plumbago capensis* |
| *Bougainvillea* | |

# Ferns

You can grow any number of ferns in a greenhouse. They do particularly well on a north-facing side, which is shady and moist. Some ferns which should thrive are:

| | |
|---|---|
| *Adiantum cuneatum* | *Pteris cretica 'Albolineata'* |
| *Adiantum decorum* | *Pteris cretica 'Major'* |
| *Adiantum elegans* | *Pteris tremula* |
| *Cyrtomium falcatum* (Holly fern) | *Pteris wimsetti* |

Ferns can be propagated in several ways. Many can be successfully grown from spores, but the fern *Asplenium bulbiferum* can be multiplied from small, bulb-like structures called bulbils. Other ferns throw out runners from which new plants can be cultivated. A fern easily propagated in this way is *Nephrolepis* in which miniature plants are produced at the ends of the runners. These will grow independently if merely pegged down into the earth where they will root.

# Greenhouse Pot Plants (Flowering Plants)

| GENUS | SPECIES etc. | EASE OF CULTURE | PROPAGATION | FLOWERING TIME | AVERAGE HEIGHT | TEMP. REQ. | NOTES |
|---|---|---|---|---|---|---|---|
| ACHIMENES | (various colours) | T | Rhizomes (tubers) March/April | May-Sept. | 6-9 in. | I | Dry out rhizomes over winter |
| APHELANDRA | squarrosa 'Louisae' | T | Cuttings, various times. Use propagation case | Various | 12-16 in. | H | Can be difficult to grow and dislikes damp or draughts |
| AZALEA | indica | D | Cuttings in spring in propagation case | Xmas on | 12-16 in. | C/I | Grafted plants can be retained for years |
| BEGONIA | semperflorens / Tuberous (double) / 'Gloire de Lorraine' | T / E / E | Seed Feb./onwards / Start tubers February / Cuttings mid-August / Cuttings Feb./onwards | June-Sept. / June-Sept. / November-February | 6-12 in. / 12-15 in. / 9-12 in. | I / I / I | Tubers rest in winter |
| BELOPERONE | guttata (Shrimp Plant) | D | Cuttings in April in propagating case | Summer | 12-16 in. | I | Likes a little shade in summer. Give plenty of water |
| CACTI | various types | E/T | Various methods. Sections of stems etc., also seed | Various | Various | C/I | Dozens of different types. Most can be grown in frost-free greenhouse in J.I.+grit. Give plenty of sun |
| CALCEOLARIA | herbeohybrida (hybrida multiflora) multiflora nana | T / T | Seed in July/August | March-May | 12-16 in. | C | Cool steady growth. Put in 5-6 in. pots for flowering |
| CAMELLIA | japonica | D | Leaf bud cuttings March. Pot in 6 in. pots | Winter/Early Spring | 18-24 in. | C | Lime-free compost essential. Stand in cold frame in summer |
| CAMPANULA | isophylla var. alba | E | Cuttings in March | Summer | Pendulous | C | Ideal for hanging baskets or edge of staging |
| CAPSICUM (grown for decorative fruit) | annuum | T | Seed in February | Autumn on | 10-12 in. | C | Keep cool. Shade if necessary. Spray frequently when flowering to assist fruit formation |
| CELOSIA | argentea cristata pyramidalis | E | Seed in February | May-Sept. | 15 in. | C | A fairly simple plant to grow. Gives good colour and lots of interest |

Key  D = Difficult; E = Easy; T = Tricky.

C = Cool; I = Intermediate; H = Hot.

| CHRYSANTHEMUMS (in pots) | | See Chapter 7 | | | | | |
|---|---|---|---|---|---|---|---|
| CINERARIA | grandiflora, multiflora, multiflora nana | T | Seed May/June | Spring on | 12–15 in. | C | Place outside in summer in shaded position. Keep cool in greenhouse not above 55 °F. Best on slatted open bench |
| CRASSULA | (Rochea) coccinea | E | Cuttings in Spring | June on | 9–10 in. | C | Add lime to compost. Cold frames in summer |
| CYCLAMEN | persicum | D | Seed space sown (120 seeds per tray) September-January. Pot early and keep corm above soil level. Corms can be potted in August | August on | 9–10 in. | C | Flowers in 5–6 in. pot. Cold frame or cool greenhouse in summer. Regular feeding essential |
| ECHEVERIA | retusa | E | Sections of stem with rosette of leaves after flowering | Winter | 9–10 in. | C/I | A relatively easy plant to grow, but dislikes overwatering |
| ERICA (Heath) | gracilis, gracilis alba, nivalis, hyemalis, willmorei | T | Tip of stem cuttings, $\frac{3}{4}$ in. long, in November/January. Root in 3 parts peat, 1 part sand in propagating case | Throughout Winter | 12–18 in. | C | Lime-free compost (J.I.+flowers of sulphur, without lime). Stop frequently to encourage bushy growth. Takes 2 years to develop. Plant outside during second season |
| FUCHSIA | fulgens (many different varieties) | E | Internodal cuttings January/February in individual containers. Root in propagating case | Summer/ Autumn | Various | C | Frequent feeding essential. Give plenty of air and water in later stages of growth. Stake. Bad for fly |
| GENISTA | (Cytisus canariensis) | E | Cuttings January/April. Takes 2 years to produce good plant | Spring | 12–24 in. | C | Really a shrub. Merely requires cool growing and regular trimming to keep bushy. Stand outside and keep shaded during second season. Lift in for winter |

| Name | | Propagation | Flowering period | Height | Temp | Notes |
|---|---|---|---|---|---|---|
| GERANIUM (Zonal Pelargonium) (Regal Pelargonium) Many lovely varieties, the new Irene strain has prolific blooms. Ivy-leaved, especially for hanging baskets. Scented, variegated | E | Cuttings at various times of year. Autumn or spring. Individual containers or open propagating bench | Long flowering period | Various | C | One of the easiest plants to grow. Do not overwater and keep feeding |
| GLOXINIA | T | Seed in January/February. Tubers, leaf cuttings mid-April in propagating case | August/September | 9–12 in. | I | Needs constant watering and feeding |
| HIPPEASTRUM (Amaryllis) | T | Pot bulb in 5–6 in. pot for starting in Spring, December or earlier | Xmas/Spring | 18–20 in. | I | |
| HYDRANGEA macrophylla (Many excellent varieties) | D | Internodal stem cuttings February/May (non-flowering shoots only). Trim leaves to reduce transpiration loss | Spring | 16–20 in. or taller | C/I | Stand outside in summer, or in cold frame. Pinch plant to encourage leaf growth. Keep nitrogen and phosphate levels low during feeding. Use iron sequestrine if foliage turns white. Apply blueing compound to intensify blue colour |
| IMPATIENS sultanii (Busy Lizzie) | E | Seed February/March or cuttings at various times | Summer | 10–15 in. | C/I | A very simple plant to grow. Must have plenty of light |
| MARGUERITE (Crysanthemum frutescens) (white) (C. coronarium (yellow)) | E | Cuttings August/January. Seed February | Summer | 12–16 in. | C | Keep cool. Stop frequently to induce bushy plant |
| POINSETTIA (Euphorbia pulcherrima) | D | Stem cuttings in May | Autumn/Winter | 2–4 ft. | C/I | Stand in frame August/September and avoid dryness. Grown for coloured bracts |
| POLYANTHUS | E | Seed in May. Pot into 3½ in. pots | Early Spring on | 9–12 in. | C | Stand in frame during summer. Keep cool and well watered. Lift into greenhouse December onwards |

| | | | | | | | |
|---|---|---|---|---|---|---|---|
| PRIMULA | obconica malacoides kewensis sinensis | E | Seed sown thickly May-June. Pot into 5 in. pot | Spring/Summer | 9–12 in. | C | Keep dry in winter till flowering starts. Apply iron sequestrine if yellowing of foliage occurs. Note: Many people are allergic to Primulas, (cause a rash) |
| ROSES | dwarf types | T | Buy in and pot in 5 in. pots December/January and cut hard back | Summer | 16–18 in. | C/I | The object is merely to advance flowering. Use any good compost and keep feeding |
| SAINTPAULIA | ionantha | T | Seed in Spring (do not come true from seed). Leaf stalk cuttings. Shade from direct light | Flower over a long period | 6–9 in. | I/H | Feed regularly with high potash feed. Keep well watered and warm. Avoid draughts |
| SALPIGLOSSIS | | T | Seed in September | May | 2–3 ft. | C | Grow cool |
| SALVIA | 'Blaze of Fire', 'Harbinger' | E | Seed in January/February. Flowers in 5-in. pot | Summer | 9–12 in. | C | Really a bedding plant, but excellent in pots. Keep cool in Summer |
| SCHIZANTHUS | (Poor Man's Orchid) | T | Seed August | April/May | 12–24 in. | C | Grow cool. Give plenty of light and adequate support. Pinch out to ensure bushy growth |
| SCHLUMBERGERA X | buckleyi (Xmas Cactus) | E | Sections of stem segments in spring | Xmas on | pendulous | C | Keep cool in summer. Give plenty of water. Repot occasionally |
| SOLANUM | capsicastrum, pseudocapsicum (attractive berries) | D | Seed in February. Sow 150 per tray. Cuttings in February in propagating case | Winter, especially Xmas | 12–16 in. | I | Stand in shady frames in summer, lifting out during September. Always add Epsom salts, $\frac{3}{4}$ oz. per bushel. Stop plant height to induce bushy growth. Syringe frequently during flowering to induce setting. Save seed of good forms |
| STOCKS | Beauty of Nice | E | Seed July/August | Spring | 18 in. | C | Keep cool and airy |
| STREPTOCARPUS | | T | Seed January/March. Leaf cuttings in August | August/October | 9 in. | C | Feed and water regularly |
| ZANTEDESCHIA | aethiopica (Arum) | T | Division in July/August | Easter on | 2–3 ft. | C/I | Rest outdoors in summer before repotting |

# Greenhouse Pot Plants (Foliage Plants)

| GENUS | SPECIES etc. | PROPAGATION | HEIGHT | TEMP. | NOTES |
|---|---|---|---|---|---|
| ARALIA (Fatsia) | Fatsia japonica | Root cuttings in March | 2–3 ft. | C | Green healthy fig-like leaves |
| BEGONIA | rex (Many other types) | Leaf or stem cuttings anytime in propagating case | 12–24 in. and taller | I | Water sparingly in Winter |
| CHLOROPHYTUM | conosum variegatum (spider plant) | Layer small plantlets to ground | 12–18 in. | C | Easy plant to grow |
| CISSUS | antarctica (Kangaroo Vine) | Leaf bud or terminal cuttings | 12–18 in. | I | An excellent foliage plant. Keep well supported |
| COLEUS | blumei (Many colour forms) | Seed – Variable colours. Cuttings rooted in propagating case in Spring | 1–2 ft. | I | Must have plenty of light. Keep well watered |
| CROTON | Codiaeum variegatum | Cuttings with at least 6–7 leaves. Also leaf bud cuttings. Both in propagating case | 1–2 ft. | I | Give full light and keep cool. Shade only in full sun |
| DIEFFENBACHIA | picta (Dumb Cane) | Terminal and stem cuttings, the latter with 2 buds horizontally. Both in propagating case | 1–2 ft. | I | A fairly easy plant to grow |
| DRACAENA | (inc. Cordyline) | Stem cuttings. Cordyline australis and C. terminalis from seed February/March | 18 in. | I | Shade and high humidity necessary |
| FATSHEDERA | (a cross between Fatsia japonica and Hedera helix) | Terminal and leaf bud cuttings in propagating case | 18–24 in. | I | Must be well supported |
| FICUS | elastica 'Decora', lyrata (Fiddle-leaf fig) pumila | Leaf bud and terminal cuttings in propagating case | 1–2 ft. | I/H | Not the easiest plant to grow |
| GREVILLEA | robusta (Silk Oak) | Seed November/March | 2 ft. | I | Cool and shade required |
| HEDERA | (the ivies) | Tips or leaf cuttings any time | Trailing | I | Easy to grow. Ideal for edge of staging |

| | | | | | |
|---|---|---|---|---|---|
| MARANTA | leuconeura kerchoviana | Division of roots in Spring | 1–2 ft. | I | Easily grown |
| PEPEROMIA | argyreia (sandersii) hederifolia tithymaloides 'Variegata' | Leaf bud cuttings or leaf blade sections | 9–12 in. | I | Easy to cultivate |
| PHILODENDRON | (Various species and number of related plants such as Scindapsus aureus and Monstera deliciosa) | Leaf bud or terminal stem cuttings. All in propagating case | 12–16 in. | I | Needs support, shade from sun |
| PILEA | cadierei | Nodal or terminal cuttings in propagating case | 9–12 in. | I | An easy plant to grow |
| RHOICISSUS | rhomboidea (Grape Ivy) | Leaf bud or heeled cuttings in propagating case | 12–24 in. | I | Needs support |
| RICINUS | communis (Castor Oil Plant), (red) gibsonii, (red) sanguinea, (green) zanzibarensis | Seed in February/March | 2–3 ft. | I | Give plenty of light |
| SANSEVIERIA | trifasciata (Mother-in-Law's Tongue or Bowstring Hemp) | Cuttings from leaf tip or suckers (variegated types) | 16–18 in. | I | An indestructible plant. Easy to grow |
| SAXIFRAGA | stolonifera (Mother-of-Thousands) | Runners, root separating, or from seed | 3 in. | C | One of the easiest plants to grow |
| SELAGINELLA | (Many different types) | Cuttings | 4–6 in. | I | A useful plant for greenhouse staging |
| TRADESCANTIA | (Various kinds including Zebrina—Wandering Sailor) | Cuttings | Trailing | I | Easily grown plant with variegated leaves. Ideal for edge greenhouse staging |

77

# 5 Bulb Forcing

## Choosing and planting bulbs – daffodils – tulips – crocuses – gladioli – hyacinths – irises – freesias

Although it need not be done in a greenhouse, bulb forcing is a hobby which offers any gardener plenty of scope for producing showy flowers in large numbers and well before outdoor bulbs have burst into bloom. Bulbs are easy to deal with, and need little or no artificial heat, but do select renowned, reliable suppliers. High-class bulbs cost little more than poor-quality specimens, yet the extra money is a good insurance against disappointment.

## Choosing and planting bulbs

The bulbs which will flower the earliest are usually specially treated by the growers and can be bought ready planted in bowls full of fibre or can be planted in soil in boxes or pots in your own greenhouse, with the tip of the bulb just showing. Bed down hyacinths in September, tulips and daffodils in October.

Because rooting is quickest and most prolific at low temperatures, put the planted bulbs in a cold frame, a sheltered corner of the garden or cellar and insulate them with a covering of moist peat or cold ashes. They are unlikely to need watering, but if the weather is very dry, give the peat an occasional, but thorough hosing.

Once the growing shoots are green and have pushed well above ground, so that $1\frac{1}{2}$–2 in. are showing, lift the bulbs into a warm greenhouse – it should be between 55 and 60 °F. At first, keep tulips and hyacinths in the dark, daffodils in the light. After 7–10 days, when the flower stems are well lengthened, give them more heat and full light either in the greenhouse or in your house. Later flowering bulbs can, however, be brought straight into the light, but whichever method you choose, always make sure that the bulbs do not dry out.

Many bulbs, but particularly tulips and daffodils do well if planted in greenhouse borders. There they will give you cut flowers early on in the year. For pot-planted bulbs, an alternative to bringing them out from darkness to daylight is to force them to flower in artificial light at a temperature of 65–70 °F. A warm cellar or cupboard is ideal for the purpose. For every square yard of space you will need one 100 watt bulb. Switch these lights on for 12 hours in every 24. The greatest disadvantage of forcing bulbs in artificial light is that they tend, especially daffodils, to sprout too many leaves and not enough flowers.

**Daffodils.** One of the largest and least troublesome of groups, the daffodils or narcissi offer a greenhouse gardener an enormous choice. For the earliest flowers, choose well-established varieties like 'Paper White' and Grand Monarch. For later on, the Barrie, King Alfred and Trumpet groups are probably the gems of the whole family.

Pot up daffodils and narcissi in a rich compost of $\frac{3}{4}$ leaf mould and $\frac{1}{4}$ peat moss. Keep them insulated in peat or ashes, in the dark, until the spears of the leaves look green and you can feel the flower bud clear of the neck of the bulb, then give them constant light and air. By November, the early flowerers will need some warmth, while the rest will appreciate a rise in temperature from December through to March. Avoid intense heat until the bud is fully out of the bulb. Always stake daffodils and narcissi well to stop them bending and breaking.

**Tulips**, in myriad varieties, growing in number year by year, will flower in pots from Christmas until the end of May. For old-established favourites, choose Prince of Austria, and General de Wet to bloom earlier, followed by Mendel, Triumph and finally Darwins. Pot your early varieties in September, in light, sandy soil. The later ones can wait until November and prefer a good loam.

Force your early tulips by plunging them into peat. As soon as the flower buds appear they can have constant light. The later sorts will probably not need darkening and will develop naturally with very little heat.

**Crocuses.** Most members of the crocus family flower early and if planted in good time – in September or October – will bloom in January or February, or even at Christmas. After planting, cover the pots with peat or ashes for five weeks, then keep them in a cold frame until December or January when you can bring them into the warmth. Try to avoid sharp temperature changes, especially from cold to hot. They will make the foliage grow long and spindly and the blooms may fail.

**Gladioli.** These beautiful corms will flower much earlier in the greenhouse than out-of-doors, but you cannot force them as hard as tulips or daffodils. For the best results, put them in greenhouse borders filled with a rich loam, 6 in. apart and 3 in. below the soil surface in February or March. Or put the largest ones in 8- or 9-in. pots. Allard Pierson is an excellent early-flowerer, and is one of the popular primulinus group.

# Bulbs for Forcing

## Daffodils

FOR CHRISTMAS. 'Paper White', 'Grand Soleil d'or'.

JANUARY ONWARDS. 'Barrie', 'King Alfred', 'Mrs. R. O. Blackhouse', 'February Gold', 'Cheerfulness', 'Silver Chimes', 'Polar Ice'.

## Hyacinths

BLUE. 'King of the Blues' (deep blue), 'Ostara' (deep blue, very early), Lilac 'Amethyst' (violet).

PINK AND RED. 'Gipsy Queen' (tangerine), 'Jan Bos'

(bright red), 'Pink Pearl' (deep pink), 'Scarlet Perfection' (double scarlet).

WHITE. 'Carnegie' (pure white), 'L'Innocence' (pure white, large bells).

YELLOW. 'Prins Hendrik' (clear yellow), 'Yellow Hammer' (golden yellow, early).

MINIATURES. 'Vanguard' (light blue, early).

## Tulips

EARLY. 'Brilliant Star' (scarlet), 'Prince of Austria' (orange-scarlet), 'Sunburst' (yellow).

EARLY DOUBLE. 'Dante' (blood red), 'Electra' (cherry-red), 'Mr. Van der Hoef' (rich yellow).

EARLY DARWINS. 'Kansas' (white), 'Glory of Noordwijk' (rose-pink), 'Elmus' (red edged white).

COTTAGE. 'Dreaming Maid' (white edged violet), 'Marshall Haig' (scarlet yellow centre), 'Palestrina' (pink inside, green outside).

**Hyacinths.** With a little forethought, you should be able to have these heady-scented flowers in bloom for Christmas. Pot Roman hyacinths in late August or early September and keep them under a peat pile for about 5 weeks. By November you should be able to bring them into a slightly-warmed greenhouse in full light. Following Roman hyacinths, plant other varieties to give a good show right through until April.

**Irises.** Like gladioli, irises can be planted in the spring, but there are many varieties which will give you colour in the months of March and April if planted in the autumn. Do not force these irises, but plant them in borders or pots in the greenhouse and leave them to develop naturally in its sheltered environment. Set them about 3 in. deep and 3–4 in. apart. The varieties Wedgewood and Imperator are best for autumn planting.

**Freesias.** Many people count freesias as their favourite flowers – their scent is delicious, their blooms are bright but delicate. Thanks to modern plant breeding, freesias come in a wonderful range of colours. You can either grow freesias from

81

Pot-grown hyacinths like these are amongst the most attractive of bulbs for indoor decoration in the winter. They should be started in the greenhouse in November.

seed or from corms. Sow seed in April, plant the corms in August or September.

Freesia corms thrive in a loamy soil and need plenty of ventilation. Until growth starts, cover the pots with an inch of moss, but remove it as soon as the leaves start to show, so that they can grow unhindered. At this stage, they can be taken into the greenhouse, but do not let them get too hot – a place near the glass is ideal.

There are three main methods of growing freesias from seed. Firstly, the seeds can be sown in boxes of moist peat, covered with a sheet of glass and paper and kept at a temperature of 55–60 °F. Once the germination process is complete, the seedlings can be pricked off, 2 in. apart, into 9-in. clay or bituminized pots made of tough paper, filled with John Innes

Daffodils can be grown in bowls in the greenhouse for bringing indoors for decoration.

No. 2 or U/C summer mix compost. Secondly, the seeds can be sown direct in the containers, but in this case, germination does tend to be erratic. Thirdly, you can sow the seeds individually into peat blocks, which can then be planted in pots or in greenhouse borders, but this method takes up a lot of greenhouse space and the foliage is far more prolific than the flowers.

During the summer months, take the young plants, in boxes or pots, out into a cold frame. Fed and watered regularly, they should make good growth. In September, take the plants back to the greenhouse. With water and moderate warmth they will soon flower, and will give you many weeks of colour. Help prevent the plants flopping and breaking by staking them to stout twigs.

# 6 Raising Summer Bedding Plants

## Plants in the greenhouse – propagation

Although many gardeners take the lazy way out and buy summer bedding plants from their local nurseries, there is much more satisfaction in growing your own plants, either from cuttings or from seed. And as well as a sense of achievement, you will be able to grow just the colours and varieties you want. The greenhouse is exactly the right place to give these plants a good start in life.

## Plants in the greenhouse

Summer bedding plants which need special care are dahlias and begonias, as neither will tolerate the slightest frost. Start the cuttings into growth by bedding the respective corms or tubers in moist peat during February and March, and giving plenty of warmth. Conventional cuttings can then be taken and rooted normally. Or you can store the tubers and corms in a frost-free place over the winter and plant them out or pot them in late April or early May, when they should grow naturally.

After they have overwintered in a frost-free greenhouse, many plants such as *Centaurea* or *Salvia* can be divided in spring. Use a sharp knife to split the plants, then pot them up in separate pots containing a high-quality compost.

The easiest and most common way of raising bedding plants is direct from seed. You will have to plant these seeds at different times, as some take longer to develop then others. For good measure, sow one seed pan of each species you select. As they grow, prick the seedlings off into boxes or containers with many separate compartments. Watch out for damping off – a fungal attack on the seedlings. Once it starts it will spread through a whole batch of seedlings very rapidly and there is little you can do to stop it. This is particularly common in lobelias and antirrhinums, but is made worse by loam which has been sterilized at high temperatures, for this soil gives off ammonia which, in turn, encourages the growth of the fungus. For this reason, choose a soil-free growing medium such as a peat-based preparation.

The whole spectrum of bedding plants contains, as you might expect, some perennials, some annuals, some hardy, others half-hardy or tender. For convenience, all can be given the same kind of treatment. Your aim should be to have them ready to set out in the garden as soon as the spring displays are over, probably in mid-May, though the exact time will vary from district to district and possibly from year to year. In northern areas, or if plants are very tender, be patient and wait until late May before you expose your carefully-tended greenhouse plants to the rigours of the weather.

# Propagation

Although you will want to synchronize your timing, different bedding plants will need different treatments. Seeds are easy, and should present you with few problems, but taking cuttings can be more tricky. These cuttings can either be taken from hardy or half-hardy perennials in September to October or taken from the same plants before they are lifted out of their summer beds. As a third alternative, you can take cuttings in the spring from plants which have been overwintered in a frost-free greenhouse, though some, such as pentstemons and marguerites are, in fact, tolerant of freezing temperatures.

Clip off sturdy cuttings 3 or 4 in. long and, preferably, though not necessarily, without flowers. Trim them, and place them 2 in. apart in boxes containing a rooting medium of sand, peat

Dahlia tubers should be started in a box of peat in the greenhouse in early spring.

Dahlia tubers should be washed clean and stored in almost dry peat.

and a little clean soil. A frost-free greenhouse will now come into its own, for although the cuttings may survive, root and grow in a sheltered cold frame or with a sack draped over them, the greenhouse will prevent massive losses of cuttings as the result of frost, snow and damp.

Do not struggle or be impatient for quick growth. Large plants, produced too soon will be a nuisance rather than an asset. In the same way you can take your time with cuttings from plants which have been overwintered in the greenhouse. But in this case you can encourage the cuttings to root more quickly by keeping them in a warm place, either in boxes or on a warm propagating bench. During the early part of the year, once strong growth begins, take the cuttings out of the greenhouse and put them into good soil in a cold frame or, if they are exceptionally hardy, like pentstemons or geraniums, into individual 4-in. pots. For geraniums use John Innes potting compost, U/C summer mix, or some other suitable potting compost. To make for strong growth, put them into a place in the greenhouse which gets a good light.

PLANTS FOR SUMMER BEDDING

| NAME | PROPAGATION | COLOUR | HEIGHT | DIST. APART |
|------|-------------|--------|--------|-------------|
| AGERATUM | Seed in February/March | Blue | 4–9 in. | 6 in. |
| ALYSSUM | Seed in February/March | White, pink | 4–6 in. | 6 in. |
| ANTIRRHINUM | Seed in February/March | Various | 12–18 in. | 10–12 in. |
| ASTER, China | Seed in March | Various | 12–18 in. | 10–12 in. |

| | | | | |
|---|---|---|---|---|
| **BEGONIA** (Fibrous rooted) | Sow seed or take cuttings of overwintered plants in spring | Various | 9–12 in. and higher | 9–12 in. |
| **BEGONIA** (Tuberous) | By division of tubers after start of growth in spring or by seed in February/March | Various | 9–12 in. or more | 9–12 in. |
| **CALCEOLARIA** | By cuttings in autumn or spring | Red and yellow | 12–15 in. | 9 in. |
| **CARNATION** (Marguerite or Chabaud) | Seed by spring. Alternatively by cuttings or by layering during previous summer | Various | 12–14 in. | 12 in. |
| **DAHLIA** | Seeding in spring for dwarf bedding types, or cuttings from overwintered tubers when growth starts. Tubers may also be planted. | Various | 1–6 ft. | 1–3 ft. (bedding types at 1 ft. apart) |
| **DIANTHUS** | Seed in February | Various | 12–15 in. | 10–12 in. |
| **FUCHSIA** | Cuttings taken in spring | Red, pink, purple | 18 in.–3 ft. | 18 in.–3 ft. |
| **GERANIUM** (Zonal Pelargonum) | From cuttings taken in spring or autumn | Pink, white, red | 9–12 in. (also trailing types) | 9–12 in. |
| **GLADIOLUS** | By corms planted direct or started in heat prior to planting outside in May | Vast range of colours | $1\frac{1}{2}$–3 ft. or more | 6–12 in. |
| **HELIOTROPE** | By cuttings taken in spring | Blue | 9 in.–3 ft. | 1–3 ft. |
| **LOBELIA** | Cuttings may be taken in spring, but usually seed is sown in February | Blue, white, pink | 6–9 in. | 6–9 in. |
| **MARIGOLD** (French & African) | Seed sown by February/March | Orange shades | 9 in.–$2\frac{1}{2}$ ft. | 12–15 in. |
| **MESEMBRYAN-THEMUM** | From cuttings or by seed sown in spring | Various | Trailing | 9–12 in. |
| **MIMULUS** | Seed in February/March | Yellows | 12–15 in. | 10–12 in. |
| **NEMESIA** | Seed in February/March | Various | 9–12 in. | 12 in. |
| **NICOTIANA** | Seed in February/March | Shades of white, pink etc. | 12–18 in. | 12 in. |
| **PENTSTEMON** | By cuttings taken in spring or autumn | Various | 1–2 ft. | 12 in. |
| **PETUNIA** | Seed in February/March | Various | 12–15 in. | 12 in. |
| **PHLOX** (drummondii) | Seed in spring | Various | 12–15 in. | 10–12 in. |
| **SALVIA patens** | By division cuttings in spring | Blue | $1\frac{1}{2}$–2 ft. | 10–12 in. |
| **SALVIA (Scarlet)** | Preferably by seed in February, but also by cuttings | Scarlet | 1–2 ft. | 9 in. |
| **TAGETES** | Seed in February/March | Orange/Yellow | 10–12 in. | 9–12 in. |
| **VERBENA** | Cuttings in spring or by seed in January/February | Various | Trailing | 12 in. |

# 7 Chrysanthemums

## The needs of chrysanthemums – chrysanthemum types – the growth of cuttings – propagation

For producing flowers in autumn and winter, chrysanthemums are absolutely unbeatable and deserve a place in every greenhouse. Even the most inexperienced of greenhouse gardeners will get enormous fun from growing chrysanthemums and his living-rooms can be full of colour right through until Christmas.

## The needs of chrysanthemums

Although chrysanthemums can, of course be grown out-of-doors, the greenhouse is essential if you want blooms after the winter frosts have set in. Rather than planting seeds, the best way to grow chrysanthemums is from cuttings and, while these will survive in a cold frame, the greenhouse does offer a much more risk-free environment.

Chrysanthemums are interesting plants because, except for some early varieties, they will only form flower buds when the days are short. So unless there are less than $14\frac{1}{2}$ hours of daylight in every 24, you will get no buds or blooms. Botanically, chrysanthemums are perennials, and the part lodged below ground, the rootstock, is extremely hardy and resistant. Flowers and foliage, too, can stand fairly low temperatures, but much depends on type and variety. Though outdoors chrysanthemums can only be grown in the months between spring and autumn, in a greenhouse they will flourish all the year round, but without shading they will naturally only flower in the weeks when the days are short.

# Chrysanthemum types

Because there are so many chrysanthemum varieties, and because new ones are contantly appearing, it is difficult to be specific about the best sorts to grow. Rather, find a good catalogue from a specialist chrysanthemum grower and make your own choice of sizes and colour schemes. Visit flower shows, local and national, to get an idea of what is going on or join a Chrysanthemum Society to hear the latest in varieties and growing methods.

From all the variety of shape and form, experts often divide chrysanthemums into seven different types:

**Incurved.** In these chrysanthemums, all the petals turn inwards to make a ball-shaped flower.

**Incurving.** The petals of these flowers are much looser and do not form a tight ball.

**Reflexing.** In these flowers, the petals droop or turn outwards.

**Singles.** Rather than a conventional flower with many rows of petals, singles have a central eye surrounded by a single ring of petals.

**Anemone flowering.** These chrysanthemums are like singles, but the central eye is raised like an anemone.

**Large exhibition** chrysanthemums have immense flowers. They can be incurved, incurving or reflexed, but all must be grown in a greenhouse. Other chrysanthemums have varying blooms and can flower early, mid-year or late.

If you try to economize when buying stock, you may well be disappointed, so do spend the extra money on ensuring good quality. Throughout the year, keep an eye on the plants and quell any disease as soon as it appears. Plan your chrysanthemum show from year to year. The best time to choose stock for taking cuttings is when the plants are in full flower, but do not hesitate to reject any plants which have the slightest sign of distorted flowers, weak growth or mottled leaves.

To grow chrysanthemums in the greenhouse, you will want to be able to keep the temperature at a minimum of 45 or 50 °F to get autumn and winter flowers. Good light is a must, and you will need a bench – either slatted or solid with a capillary watering system – if you plan to grow chrysanthemums in pots. To harden off your cuttings, a frame is a good idea, but not essential.

## The growth of cuttings

As they grow, your chrysanthemum cuttings will produce several shoots, but you can manipulate the plant to produce the kind of flowers you want. If you want several large, single blooms on each plant, completely remove the tops of the single stems when 6–9 in. of growth has been achieved and the buds are beginning to break. Done carefully, without bruising the plant, this will encourage side shoots to grow. After this, you can take off all but the central bud on each side shoot.

The only chrysanthemums which do not need this stopping or pinching process are the spray varieties which, left untampered with, produce enormous numbers of small, starry blossoms. One word of warning: do not stop chrysanthemums at the same time as you are moving them. This is too much of a shock. Instead, wait until the plants are well established in their new positions.

There are three main methods of chrysanthemum-growing to choose from, each with its advantages, but the one you select will probably depend on the varieties you choose.

**Pots.** In this method, chrysanthemum cuttings are first rooted in boxes then transferred to 3-in. pots, followed by 5-in., then 8- or 9-in. pots in which they mature and flower. The 5-in. pots are best filled with John Innes No. 2 compost, but add plenty of crocks and a layer of rough fibrous material such as rough peat at the bottom of the pot to give good drainage. For the final potting in the largest-size pots, use John Innes No. 3 compost and an extra thick layer of roughage.

To stop the larger plants from keeling over, put three or four strong canes, each about four feet long, round the edge of each pot and tie twine between them. For a few days, put the pots in a square to give them plenty of natural protection, then arrange them in a line along the greenhouse wall at 6-in. intervals. Give regular water and liquid feed, and turn the pots from time to time to make sure each plant gets even light and so that the roots do not grow out of the pot and into the ground.

**Lifting.** In the lifting process, the chrysanthemum cuttings

Chrysanthemums are an ideal greenhouse crop. The modern strains can be had in flower at all times of the year.

are first established in pots then lifted into borders inside the greenhouse. The best time for this lifting operation is September or early October, well before the winter frosts set in. At this stage, you will probably have the young plants in 5- or 9-in. pots (for details see the previous section), or growing in good rich soil outdoors in a sheltered spot or cold frame.

For good results, it is worth the trouble of preparing the greenhouse thoroughly before putting the chrysanthemums inside. Fork over the soil in the borders and add 4–6 oz. of a good general fertilizer to every square yard. Using a spade, and keeping as much soil as possible round the roots of each plant, lift the chrysanthemums into the border. Water them well. Over the next few days you may notice some wilting, but the plants will recover quickly as long as you keep the greenhouse cool. After a couple of weeks, heat the greenhouse to the 45–50 °F mark.

**Direct planting.** Though a great favourite with commercial chrysanthemum growers, direct planting is often a nuisance for amateurs because it takes up so much greenhouse space. This, in turn, means that if you choose the direct-planting method, you will only be able to squeeze in an early crop of tomatoes. Because they develop much more quickly in the greenhouse, there is no need to put in chrysanthemum plants until well into the summer. Choose your time, from mid-June to mid-August.

Another difficulty of direct planting is that it may be difficult to grow, or obtain, cuttings which are at the right stage of maturity. One good idea is to take cuttings early in the year, to establish them in the greenhouse, stop them when they are growing vigorously by pinching out the tops, then taking another set of cuttings and rooting those.

Chrysanthemums planted direct will do best if kept at a constant temperature of 55–60 °F, especially when the buds are forming in September and October and, of course, regularly fed and watered. When feeding, concentrate particularly on nitrogen and potassium, and make sure the greenhouse is well aired. Support the plants well and allow plenty of space – a maximum of 10 in. – between each.

# Propagation

Plan your propagation programme well in advance, so that

you are ready to take cuttings at the right time of year. Take cuttings of large, exhibition greenhouse chrysanthemums in December and January, of late-flowering and those which bloom in the middle of the season in February and March, and of early-flowering chrysanthemums in March and April.

Select your cuttings from plants which have spent the winter in a protected frame or frost-free greenhouse. From below a joint, take each cutting 2–3 in. long and about $\frac{1}{8}$ in. in diameter. Always strip off the lower leaves, then dip the cuttings in hormone powder. For rooting, make up a mixture of equal amounts of peat and sand and put in the cuttings $\frac{1}{2}$–$\frac{3}{4}$ in. deep and 1–1$\frac{1}{2}$ in. apart in seed trays. Water them well, then keep them at 55–60 °F. Within a fortnight to a month, the cuttings should have rooted – you can tell when rooting is well established because the tips of the cuttings become a fresh green – but you can help speed up the process by covering the box with a sheet of polythene to keep in air and moisture, or by using a proper propagating unit. One particularly good way of propagating chrysanthemums is to put the cuttings into peat pellets, and this method is well worth considering.

Once cuttings have rooted, transfer them to 3-in. pots filled with John Innes potting compost No. 1 or some other good compost. Or you can plant them, 5 in. apart, in a good rich soil in a cold frame.

# Greenhouse Chrysanthemums

LARGE EXHIBITION. 'Duke of Kent', white, 3$\frac{1}{2}$ feet. 'Gigantic', salmon, 4$\frac{1}{2}$ feet. 'Majestic', light bronze, 3 feet. 'Shirley Primrose', yellow, 5–6 feet. 'Cossack', red, 4 feet. 'Connie Mayhew', yellow, 5 feet.

INCURVEDS. 'Audrey Shoesmith', pink, 5 feet. 'White Audrey Shoesmith', white, 5 feet. 'Lilian Shoesmith', bronze, 4 feet.

REFLEXED. 'Stuart Shoesmith', pink, 5 feet. 'Elizabeth Woolman', pink, 3 feet. 'Princess Anne', pink, 3$\frac{1}{2}$ feet. 'Woking Scarlet', red, 3$\frac{1}{2}$ feet.

SINGLES. 'Albert Cooper', yellow, 4$\frac{1}{2}$ feet. 'Broadacre', white, 3$\frac{1}{2}$ feet. 'Preference', pink 4$\frac{1}{2}$ feet. 'Woolman's Glory', bronze, 4$\frac{1}{2}$ feet.

GREENHOUSE CARNATIONS. 'Border Fancy', white, rose markings. 'Bridesmaid', pink, scarlet centre. 'Desert Song', apricot pink, with lavender-grey overlay. 'Ertrickdale', clear yellow. 'Fair Maiden', white, scarlet edge. 'Lavender Clove', lavender-grey. 'Montrose', scarlet. 'Oakfield Clove', crimson. 'White Ensign', pure white.

As long as your greenhouse is light, airy, and can be heated to 50 °F or more, it should be an excellent spot for growing carnations. There are hundreds of varieties to choose from, but the perpetual flowering Sim sports, which you can select from any good grower's catalogue, will give you the best results.

Buy young carnation plants early in the year, and arrange for them to be delivered in April. At this stage, they will be in 3-in. pots ready for moving into 6-in. pots with No. 3 John Innes compost or for planting out in beds. These beds should consist of soil raised 8 or 10 in., supported with concrete at the sides, and have drainage holes at the base.

When the plants are well established, take off the tips to encourage side shoots to grow. Once these side shoots are 5 or 6 in. long, they too can be 'stopped' so that each bears a single bud. Regular watering is a must for carnations, and an even temperature of 55–60 °F. Always avoid sharp changes of heat which will damage the plants, and give them plenty of air. As the carnations get taller, you will need to support them with canes.

As soon as you have cut your first carnations, then you can begin feeding with a well-balanced fertilizer. To keep a regular supply of stock going, take cuttings in early and late spring. This will also mean that you have a good supply of plants to replace old ones which are becoming 'leggy' and that you can ward off rusts and the red spider which are the carnation's most fierce attackers. For cuttings choose shoots well above the base of the plant and just below the flowers. Root them in sand.

# 8 Greenhouse Food Crops

**Melons – cucumbers – vines – lettuce – strawberries – french beans – peaches and nectarines – other early crops**

There are few more pleasurable sensations for a gardener than eating crops he has grown himself. And when those foods are out-of-season delicacies, then he may be justified in considering himself a gourmet. Many fruits and vegetables are easy to grow in the greenhouse and need little attention apart from routine care. More important is knowing the particular demands of each plant, and to plan your planting from season to season.

## Melons

Delicious to the taste buds, melons are extremely simple to cultivate. After you have finished your spring propagating programme, a few melon plants can be put into a bench or part of a border on the sunny side of your greenhouse.

Sow melon seeds in March or early April. Use 3-in. peat pots, and put one seed in each by pressing it in sideways. Fill the pots with John Innes No. 1 or some other good compost. During the germination process – it will take about a month for seedlings to be 6–8 in. tall and ready for planting out – you have plenty of time to prepare the permanent beds. To do this, mix a 2-ft. mound of soil with about a fifth or a sixth of its bulk composed of well-rotted manure. For every bushel of the mixture ($22 \times 10 \times$

12 in.) add an 8-oz. dressing of tomato base fertilizer, that is, medium potash. Or you can simply use John Innes No. 2 potting compost.

When the seedlings are growing strongly – in April or May – set the plants, still in their degradable peat pots, well up in the soil and give them plenty of warmth. This way they will get full light and have more resistance to disease. To encourage the side shoots to flourish, pinch out the tip of the growing shoot. These laterals can then be carefully trained to horizontal wires or a light, temporary wooden framework, such as a section of a trellis. After this, there is no need to stick to a rigid pattern. Just train the plants in the way which works out most conveniently.

To get any mature fruits, you will need to pollinate the female melon flowers by hand. Strip off the male flowers and stroke them over the female flowers, or use a soft paintbrush to transfer the pollen. Although it is a wise precaution to pollinate all the female flowers, only let four fruits develop on each plant. As these get heavier, support them with small string nets. You can buy these in garden supply shops, but they are easily made out of old netting.

From germination onwards, melons need plenty of water, plus liquid feed, and especially when the fruit is swelling. Once the fruits are fully developed, you can cut down on both. The fruit is ripe when the top responds to gentle pressure and when a sweet, heady aroma fills the greenhouse.

These are some of the best varieties to choose from:

| | |
|---|---|
| 'Best of all' | Green flesh, finely netted. |
| 'Blenheim Orange' | Delicate flavour, rich scarlet flesh. |
| 'Hero of Lockinge' | Early to mature. Prolific, white-fleshed fruits set freely. |

**Canteloupe melons.** These delicious varieties can be raised in the greenhouse then transferred to a cold frame where they will mature and bear fruits:

| | |
|---|---|
| 'Charentais' | Early medium-sized fruit. Delicious flavour, deep orange flesh. |

| 'Dutch Net or Spot' | Medium-sized fruit, free setting. |
| 'Ogen' | Early variety, small fruits. |
| 'Prescotts' | Mid-season maturer. Large fruits, scarlet flesh. |
| 'Tiger' | Early. Flat, medium-sized fruits, orange flesh. |

## Cucumbers

Like melons, their botanical relations, cucumbers are surprisingly simple to grow, and there is no need to fill the greenhouse with them, for half-a-dozen plants should supply all your salad needs. Why not try growing the early cucumber, then following this with mid- and late-season plants once your benches are free of spring cuttings.

Sow cucumber seeds from February onwards. Fill 3- or 4-in. peat pots with John Innes No. 1, or some other good-quality alternative, and press one seed sideways into each. With a greenhouse temperature of 60–65 °F, germination should take place within 48 hours. Discard any seedlings that come through later than this – they will lack vigour. When the plants are 6 or 8 in. tall, move them to 4- or 5-in. pots and support them with small stakes.

A good way of growing cucumbers is to follow the lead of the commercial suppliers and to plant them on a ridge 2 ft. high. If you do this, use equal mixtures of good loamy soil and well-rotted farmyard manure. John Innes potting compost No. 2 will give excellent results, too, but does tend to dry out rather quickly. Before you set the plants out – they should be at least 2 ft. apart – make sure that both the soil and the air in the greenhouse are at around 65 °F. Rather than carrying out elaborate schemes for training the developing cucumber plants, simply train them up strings like tomato plants or tie them to horizontal wires, but if you choose the first method you will need to cut back some of the foliage.

Throughout their growing season cucumbers need plenty of water. They love a moist, muggy atmosphere, and this is easily created by frequent spraying, but this may not be possible if you have other crops to consider. During very hot weather, you may need to shade the greenhouse glass and increase the ventilation.

When the plant roots can be seen on the surface of the ridge, top dress them with a mixture of soil and farmyard manure. Unlike melons, cucumbers set their fruits without pollination, and in fact the male flowers are best removed regularly for fertilized fruits have an unpleasant flavour.

Other ways of growing cucumbers are on straw bales, in boxes or even very large pots containing a mixture of soil and manure. For the 'bale culture' use soil and farmyard manure to make a ridge and top dress regularly with the same mixture. More details of this method can be found in the chapter on Tomatoes.

**Select your cucumbers from one of these successful varieties:**

| | |
|---|---|
| 'Best Seller' | Early maturing. Long, dark green fruits. Prolific. |
| 'Feminex' | Plants bear 100 per cent female flowers. Excellent, prolific fruits. Resistant to disease. |
| 'Bitspot' | Strong growing plants, heavy, dark green short fruits. Good disease resistance. |
| 'Green Spot' | Ribbed and spined. Excellent for both cold and heated houses. Vigorous, disease resistant. |
| 'Top Score' | Early, hardy and very prolific. Dark green medium-length fruits. Almost no male flowers. Resistant to disease. |

## Vines

The only problem likely to thwart you if you plan to grow grapes in your greenhouse is lack of space, for while vines can be small and well controlled when young, they will eventually oust all the other plants from a small house.

The ideal way to plant vines is in a special border of rotted turves fortified with plenty of bone meal and sulphate of potash. But because the roots will take up a large area, you may have to be content with planting the vines outside the greenhouse and leading the stems in through holes in the house just

Vines, although hardy themselves, seldom fruit satisfactorily out of doors. They benefit from the protected environment of the greenhouses where, with proper training, they will produce huge bunches of grapes.

Cucumbers. A far wider range of cucumbers can be grown in a greenhouse than out of doors, and they can be had in fruit over a far longer period.

above ground level. As well as giving the roots a free run, this system will be far less demanding on your water supplies.

Vine plants, which are usually called rods, are best planted in the greenhouse when two or three years old. If you are growing more than one, plant them at least three feet apart. All through the growing and fruiting season, water them well, and give balanced liquid feeds, especially when the fruits are swelling. By regulating the greenhouse temperature carefully you can pick early crops of grapes, but if you have the needs of other plants in mind, a steady temperature will merely delay ripening and probably reduce the crop. Ideally, you should start off with a temperature of 45 °F and raise this to 65 or 70 °F during the flowering season. After this, an even temperature of 65 °F gives the best results.

To prevent stressing the vines, do not pick the fruit of new rods for a year or two. It is best to take off the flowers in the first year. As the vine grows larger, trim the growing tip to fit the greenhouse conveniently. Pruning a vine can be a tricky problem and it is worth giving the problem some forethought before you wield the secateurs. In December, cut back half to two-thirds of the season's growth and trim the side shoots so that two or three plump buds remain – these buds can be easily noticed near the junction of the side shoot with the main stem. Every year, allow two new side shoots or laterals to develop at each growing point to begin with, but cut these back so that there is one lateral branching in each direction every 12 in. Tie these established laterals securely to wires. When you have decided that the rods are old enough to bear fruits, let the flower trusses form naturally then pinch off the leading shoot two leaves past the flowers. Once the fruits start to swell, thin them drastically, or you will have bunches of small, dry, bitter grapes. Vine scissors are the best implements to use. Aim for branches an inch apart within each truss.

Vine growing is often made to sound very complicated, but the secret of success in a small greenhouse is undoubtedly rigorous pruning. The largest cut-back is best done in December, though January will do, followed by ruthless cutting throughout the growing season. Vines have remarkable powers of recuperation and rarely show signs of resenting such harsh treatment.

For an amateur in Great Britain, the best variety of white grape is 'Muscal of Alexander', of black grape 'Black of Hamburg'.

# Lettuce

Lettuce has a part in the plans of nearly every keen greenhouse gardener for it is the mainstay of salads, surprisingly hardy, and quick to mature. Modern methods of plant breeding have produced a whole spectrum of varieties, some 'short day' which flourish in the dull days of winter, others 'long day' which do best in May, June and July when sunlight is at a maximum.

A good planting plan to give you lettuce for six months of the year, before your outdoor crop is ready, is set out below:

| SEED SOWING PERIOD | PLANTING IN GREENHOUSE OR FRAME | CUTTING | COMMENTS |
|---|---|---|---|
| Mid September | Mid October | December ⎫ | These are difficult crops |
| November | December | Feb.–March ⎬ | for poor light areas |
| December | January | Late March/April | |
| January | February* | April/May | |
| February | March* | May | |
| February* | Planting outside in soil blocks during March/ April | May/June | |

\* No heat needed.

There are many ways of planting lettuce seeds, but the best way is to spread them thinly in boxes containing John Innes seed compost, U/C mix or peat compost. When they are large enough, plant the seedlings out into well-dug borders dressed with tomato base fertilizer at the rate of 6–8 oz. per sq. yd. Small varieties which will mature during winter can be planted 7 in. apart, larger ones, and those needing more light, 8 in. apart. Another popular planting method is to prick out seedlings into peat 'thumb' pots and then leave them to enlarge before they are finally planted out. Always insert the young plants into damp soil and keep them well watered. For preference, use a fine mist rose on your hose pipe and begin watering when the plants have developed two or three leaves.

Water early in the day so that the plants are not wet overnight.

Although lettuce can bear the cold very well, low temperatures *will* slow growth and may make the leaves tough and bitter. Winter crops do best at a temperature of 45–50 °F, but if the thermometer tops 65 °F, which may happen in spring, make sure that you give the plants good ventilation or the tips of the leaves may burn and the plants form no hearts.

The secret of successful lettuce growing is to give them a fast, uninterrupted period of enlargement from planting to cutting. The following varieties should give good results:

### Lettuce for growing under glass:

| | |
|---|---|
| 'Amplus re-selected' | Short-day variety, forming heads winter and spring. Large leaves. Needs heat. |
| 'Cannington Forcing' | Winter variety. Smooth mid-green leaves. Resistant to some mildews. |
| 'Delta' | Medium-sized leaves. Excellent for spring crops in cold greenhouse or frame. |
| 'Kloek' | Tender green lettuce. Grow in cold or slightly heated greenhouse in autumn. Ideal for forcing under glass in spring. |
| 'Kordaat' | Specially bred for growing in a heated greenhouse in late winter. Can also be grown cold for autumn cutting. Fine round heads. |
| 'Kwiek' | Quick grower, large firm heads. Grow in cold or slightly heated greenhouse in autumn, in a slight heat in spring. |
| 'May Princess' | Attractive colour. Good head size. |
| 'Neptune' | Winter forcing variety to crop from December to March. Needs |

| | |
|---|---|
| | minimum night temperature of 45–50 °F. |
| 'Proeftuins Blackpool' | A short-day lettuce for heated greenhouses. |
| 'Profos' | Medium leaved. Fast growing for March and April picking. A short-day variety. |
| 'Toinika' | Short-day variety for February to April cutting |
| 'Valentine' | Winter forcing crop for December to March. Needs minimum night temperature of 45–50 °F. |
| 'Vitesse' | Outstanding variety. Very popular for spring cutting from heated or cool greenhouses. |

**Lettuce to sow under glass and plant out of doors:**

| | |
|---|---|
| 'All the year round' | Very hardy. Solid, pale-green heart. Crisp and tender. |
| 'Favourite' | Summer variety with large crisp heart and pale-green crimped leaves. |
| 'Trocadero Improved' | Summer or winter variety. Minimum of outside leaves. Hearts medium-sized and very compact. |
| 'Webb's Wonderful' | Summer variety. Large, solid crisp heart. Leaves well curled. |

# Strawberries

Although the forcing of strawberries is largely the province of the professional greenhouse gardener, there is nothing to stop a keen amateur from growing some strawberry plants, preferably in pots.

If you decide on strawberries as a greenhouse crop, choose healthy young runners and put them in 3-in. pots, sunk into the ground, during June and July. When the plants are large enough, re-pot them in 6-in. pots containing John Innes No. 2 potting compost, and put them on a polythene sheet in a cold frame. Except during very severe weather, these plants should need no protection until they are brought into the greenhouse in December or January.

In the greenhouse, give the strawberry plants a little water and moderate heat until they flower. At this stage, they will need a heat of 55–60 °F. Most strawberries are self-fertile, but you can dust the flowers with some cotton wool tied on a stick to ensure good pollination. Although the plants will need plenty of water, try to keep the fruit dry as it swells by supporting it on straw or with wire. Depending on the variety and the temperature in your greenhouse, you should have fruit in April or May. Some good strawberry varieties are 'Royal Sovereign', 'Cambridge Favourite', 'Templar' and, best of all for forcing, 'Gorella'.

## French beans

In a lean-to greenhouse, french beans are an ideal crop as there will be a large expanse of south-facing wall. Sow the seeds of these beans in March, into peat pots, and plant them out into a well-dug and manured border during April, 18 in. apart. To stop the stems bending and breaking, support them with string or canes and, if necessary, trim them back. Give them plenty of water, warmth and a light spraying on the morning of a sunny day.

Rather than climbers, you can grow dwarf beans in much the same way. Sow the seeds 4 or 5 to an 8-in. pot or 5 or 6 to a 10-in. pot. Half-fill each pot with John Innes potting compost No. 2. Add more compost when the plants are about 6 in. high.

Two good climbing varieties are 'Tender & True' and 'Early Bush Lake Stringless'. For dwarf plants choose 'Blue Bush Lake' or 'The Prince'.

## Peaches and nectarines

Like vines, peaches and nectarines take up a lot of greenhouse space, but are worth considering if these are your favourite fruits. A lean-to greenhouse is probably the easiest place to grow them as it has a ready-made wall.

A tree trained into a fan shape and two or three years old is the best starting point. Plant it in a well-drained loamy border and tie the branches to horizontal wires. Depending on the greenhouse temperature, flowers should form in February or March, and you can obtain good pollination with a soft paintbrush. As the miniature fruits appear, thin them out so that there is one for roughly every square foot, so that each is juicy and succulent. Plenty of water at the roots, plus daily spraying of the leaves during the morning are a must.

To train the branches of a peach or nectarine as they grow, simply tie them to your system of horizontal wires. Ruthlessly remove all badly-placed growth, especially branches which grow outwards into the greenhouse. Every autumn, you will need to cut out some of the old wood.

A good peach for an intermediate or hot house is 'Hales Early', while 'Peregrine' should do well in a cooler house. A couple of excellent nectarines are 'John Rivers' and 'Amsden June'.

## Other early crops

**Asparagus.** Lift well-developed plants into the greenhouse and pack them together under a 3-in. layer of damp peat. Then place the whole under the greenhouse shelving. With plenty of moisture plus good darkness, the shoots will quickly form.

**Rhubarb.** This is perhaps the easiest of all vegetables to force. In November, lift well-developed crowns. Let them become thoroughly frosted, trim the root ball, then pack them close together in peat. Put them under a bench where they will be in complete darkness and water them heavily. According to the greenhouse temperature, pale pink shoots will form at a steady rate.

**Sea Kale.** In the autumn, lift parent plants from your outdoor plot. Take off the side shoots and keep them for planting in the spring, then put the main plants in boxes or pots and cover them with 3 in. of good organic soil or old rotted manure. With heat, water and darkness, succulent tender shoots will form in a few weeks.

# 9 Tomatoes

**Growing methods – sowing and planting – heat, air and water – feeding – varieties to choose**

Of all greenhouse plants, tomatoes are the most popular. Any greenhouse will grow tomatoes, as long as it gets good light and is reasonably warm. There is nothing quite like the first crop of your own tomatoes – they outclass any others for flavour and quality. The better the light, the larger your tomato crop will be, but gardeners all over Britain succeed in producing high-quality tomatoes.

## Growing methods

There are six main methods of tomato-growing to choose from. Select the one that seems to suit your greenhouse and family appetites the best:

**Border culture.** In this method, tomato plants are grown in the border soil of the greenhouse. The greatest advantage of this is that it cuts down the amount of feeding and watering, but you will have to weigh this against the risk of soil deterioration caused by fungi, viruses and bacteria. In addition, there may be a lethal build-up of plant poisons and fertilizer residues. Soil borders tend to be slow to warm up in spring, the plants difficult to control.

**Grafted border plants.** One way of getting round the disadvantage of border culture is to graft normal varieties on to root stocks which are resistant to fungal diseases and one of the tomato's main enemies, the root knot eelworm. The grafting process can be difficult, so you might be well advised to buy ready-grafted plants from your local nursery if you choose this method. Though expensive, they will stay vigorous until the end of the year.

**Ring culture.** This popular method involves growing plants in 9-in. bituminized pots or rings on top of a 4–6-in. layer of weathered ashes, gravel or some other inert material. The great advantage of ring culture is that you need little fresh soil each year. The plant growth is easy to control and the small amount of growing medium fully exposed to the heat. However, the plants will need large amounts of water, especially early in the year and you have to be careful not to upset their delicate nutritional needs.

**Small amounts of growing medium.** This method is like ring culture but the plants do not stand on a gravel base. You can use a box filled with soil, a polythene bucket containing peat and vermiculite or use bituminized paper rings put on top of polythene and surrounded with a 2–3-in. layer of peat. You will need to water well all the year round.

**Straw bale culture.** In this method, straw is fermented with chemicals, placed on polythene and covered with a layer of growing medium in which the tomato plants are rooted. The polythene acts as a barrier to disease and the straw gives off both warmth and carbon dioxide which help the plants to grow. The greatest disadvantages are that the bales are space-consuming, that watering must be constant and that the plants may become over large.

**Single or double trussing.** This newest method of tomato-growing involves growing plants, each bearing only one or two trusses of fruit, in tiered troughs which are fed and watered automatically, but is really only of theoretical interest to the amateur.

## Sowing and planting

Before beginning to plant tomatoes, plan your moves carefully. Unless you have a really well-equipped greenhouse and excellent light, avoid the earliest crops. Instead, plant from mid-March to mid- or late-April to get a good crop and to economize on heating costs.

| SOWING DATE | PLANTING DATE | FIRST FRUITS RIPE |
| --- | --- | --- |
| Late November | Mid February | Mid or end of April |
| Early December | Late February | April–May |
| Late December/Early January | Mid March/Early April | Early or Mid May |
| Mid/Late February | Late April | June/July |
| Early March | Early or Mid May | July |

Sow your tomato seeds in trays or boxes, cover them lightly with compost. Water lightly and cover the seeds with a sheet of paper or paper and glass. During germination, the ideal greenhouse temperature is 65 °F. If it is higher than this, you may get 'rogue' seedlings which produce no fruits when mature.

Three or four days after germination, the seedlings will be big enough to handle and can be moved into $4\frac{1}{2}$-in. pots filled with John Innes No. 1 compost, the appropriate U/C mix or a peat compost. Keep all these young seedling plants at 63–65 °F during the day, 56–58 °F at night, but lower this two or three degrees if the *day* has been dull. High daytime temperatures increase the growth rate, but reduce the number of flowers on the bottom trusses and quicken ripening.

Keep the young plants well watered and if necessary give them a little high-potash liquid feed. When the first truss has at least one flower open they are ready for planting out. Waiting until this point is worthwhile as the fruit will set better.

Before planting out, prepare your borders or rings. Dig the borders well and if you are using fresh soil add a hundredweight of farmyard manure to every 10 or 12 sq. yds. Next, flood in lime by scattering it lightly then applying a fine mist from the hose, then, 10 or 12 days before planting, add 6 or 8 oz. of tomato base fertilizer to every square yard. This fertilizer, another John Innes standard, contains:

> two parts hoof and horn meal
> two parts superphosphates of lime
> one part sulphate of potash. .

For ring culture, the best growing medium is John Innes potting compost No. 3.

Plant your tomatoes out 20 to 24 in. apart, whether they are in borders or rings. Allow a little less for later crops, a little more for grafted plants. Make sure that the soil is damp and use a trowel to dig the hole. Do not water in too well – add just enough liquid to wet the ball of roots.

## Heat, air and water

The air temperature in the greenhouse at this stage should be about 65 °F by day and 58 °F by night. Obviously temperatures will vary, but do try to avoid very low daytime temperatures which will have a bad effect on fruit setting. The ventilators should be opened once the temperature reaches 70 to 74 °F.

Tomatoes' water needs vary a great deal with the weather. For the first few weeks after planting out, only water direct the roots of plants which wilt. A good daily spray with a fine rose will keep the atmosphere moist and encourage rooting, provided that the temperature is around 65 °F. For plants over 3 ft. tall, give the following amounts, but take care not to overwater young plants as this may stunt them.

| WEATHER | WATER/PLANT/24 HOURS |
|---------|----------------------|
| Cloudy and dull all day | $\frac{1}{4}$–$\frac{1}{2}$ pint per plant |
| Overcast most of the time | $\frac{1}{2}$–$\frac{3}{4}$ pint per plant |
| Cloudy, bright periods | $1\frac{1}{4}$–$1\frac{1}{2}$ pints per plant |
| Occasional cloud, sunny | 2–$2\frac{1}{4}$ pints per plant |
| Very sunny, clear sky all day | 3–$3\frac{1}{4}$ pints per plant |

## Feeding

There are many ways of feeding tomatoes but the best method is to look at the plant and see what it needs. Stunted plants will be short of nitrogen, lush leggy plants short of potash. So act like a doctor and prescribe according to the symptoms. This said, some gardeners feed with a 1 in 200 or 1 in 300 dilution of liquid feed at every watering: others prefer to give liquid feed every 7 or 10 days, but unless the plant looks starved, do not give any feed until the first truss of fruit is set.

Normally, tomatoes need more potash early on and more

Bottom heat is essential for the rooting of many types of cuttings and the germination of many seeds. The soil-warming cables are buried in sand and the seeds or cuttings grown in either pots or soil above the sand. The temperature is thermostatically controlled. *Courtesy of Humex.*

nitrogen later, as they use up the soil's natural nitrogen supplies. You can either buy a proprietary feed, in which case it should be used exactly as the directions advise, or you can make your own feeds containing the following substances:

| | COMPOSITION (OZ/GALL) | | | NUTRIENTS (LB/10GL) | |
|---|---|---|---|---|---|
| Potash/Nitrogen RATIO | Potassium Nitrate | Urea or | Ammonium Nitrate | $K_2O$ | N |
| 3:1 (High Potash) | 24 | — | — | 6.3 | 2.0 |
| 2:1 (Standard) | 25 | 5 | 6 | 6.3 | 3.3 |
| 1:1 (High Nitrogen) | 24 | 16 | 20 | 6.3 | 6.3 |

Remember that the ingredients will dissolve much more easily in hot water and put one fluid ounce of the solution in every $1\frac{1}{4}$ gallons of water. Apply it once every 10 to 14 days after the first truss is set, or more often, as the plant dictates. If you want to add solid feed, choose dried blood or sulphate of ammonia at 1 oz. per sq. yd.

Tomatoes are one of the most rewarding greenhouse food crops. Although not difficult to grow, they need quite a lot of attention throughout the growing season.

Plants will need support almost at once. If possible, make string loops and attach them to a wire 6 or 7 ft. above ground level or tie the plants to tall canes. Every morning or evening, nip out any side shoots. As the plant grows, carefully take off the bottom leaves to let the air circulate freely, but *only* when they are yellow or diseased. If you have limited space, pinch out the tops of the plants. To encourage surface roots to grow and to help keep the water in, give the soil a top dressing of peat or thoroughly-rotted farmyard manure.

While ring culture and border culture need similar treatment, the straw bale method makes rather special demands. For several successive days before planting, soak the bales with water. Then add $\frac{3}{4}$ lb. nitro-chalk for every 50 lb. of straw and another $\frac{1}{2}$ lb. a few days later. Then water in 9 oz. potassium nitrate and 6 oz. magnesium sulphate. Heat the bales rapidly to 110–130 °F. As the temperature falls, put in a central 6-in. ridge of John Innes potting compost No. 2. After 24 hours, put in the plants, 12–14 in. apart. Finally, feed and water as you would for other methods.

When pulling up tomato plants at the end of the season, try to remove as much of the roots as possible. Burn the spent plants as far away from the greenhouse as possible, and clean the house thoroughly to prevent diseases the next year.

## Varieties to choose

There are many different tomato varieties to choose from, and some are more disease-resistant than others. In the following tables, T/S = tall spreading; I = intermediate; C = compact. Those marked with an asterisk* are resistant to various strains of leaf mould disease.

FIRST GENERATION HYBRIDS

| | |
|---|---|
| 'AMBERLEY CROSS'*† | Early, heavy cropper (T/S). |
| 'ASIX CROSS'* | Heavy and early cropper (C). |
| 'BONSET'* | Early variety. Verticillium resistant (I). |
| 'EUROCROSS I'* | Excellent colour and quality (I). |
| 'EUROCROSS II'* | Large round fruits. Excellent for early forcing on heavy soils (I). |
| 'EUROCROSS III'* | Large many-chambered fruit. Very early heavy cropper (I). |

| | |
|---|---|
| 'FLORISSANT'* | Vigorous. Yield and quality excellent (T/S). |
| 'GLOBOSET'* | 'Ailsa Craig' type for heated or cold greenhouses (T/S). |
| 'GROWERS PRIDE'* | Early and vigorous (T/S). |
| 'HARRISONS' SYSTON CROSS'* | Short-jointed, free-setting type. Fruit of good quality and colour. Good for cool greenhouses (C). |
| 'IJSSELCROSS'* | Vigorous with larger fruit than Maascross. 'Moneymaker' type (T/S). |
| 'KINGLEY CROSS'*† | Short-jointed, high yielding (C). |
| 'MONEYGLOBE'* | Excellent quality and high yield. Free setter and earlier than 'Moneymaker' (I). |
| 'PLUSRESIST'* | Suitable for heated or cold greenhouse (I). |
| 'RIJNCROSS'* | Vigorous with well shaped fruit (T/S) |
| 'SELSEY CROSS'*† | Heavy cropper (T/S). |
| 'SERIVA'* | More vigorous and heavy cropper than 'Moneymaker'. Large fruit, (T/S). |

## DISEASE RESISTANT VARIETIES

| | |
|---|---|
| 'SUPERCROSS'* | Similar to 'Moneymaker'. Resistant to Tomato Mosaic Virus (I). |
| 'VIROCROSS'* | Resembles Supercross, but slightly larger fruit. Resistant to Tomato Mosaic Virus (I). |
| | † = Varieties bred by the Glasshouse Crops Research Institute |

## STRAIGHT VARIETIES

| | |
|---|---|
| 'AILSA CRAIG' | Fruit medium sized and well shaped (T/S). |
| 'CRAIGELLA' | 'Ailsa Craig' type (T/S). |
| 'EXHIBITION' | Heavy cropper. Even-fruited. |
| 'HARRISONS FIRST IN THE FIELD' | Good cropper. Early. |
| 'MARKET KING' | Heavy cropper. Indoor or outdoor type (T/S). |
| 'MELVILLE CASTLE' | Short-jointed. Fruit round and solid. |
| 'MINIMONK' | 'Moneymaker' type, but of compact habit (C). |
| 'MONEYCROSS' | Earlier than 'Moneymaker'. High yield. Well-shaped fruit. |
| 'MONEYMAKER' | Very popular. Medium size and good cropper. Well shaped fruit of good colour (I). |
| 'POTENTATE' | Very heavy, early cropper (I). |
| 'THE AMATEUR' | Bush variety. Suitable for cloches. Early. |

## YELLOW VARIETIES

| | |
|---|---|
| 'GOLDEN SUNRISE' | Early, medium-sized even-shaped fruit on strong trusses. |
| 'MID-DAY SUN' | Golden orange, medium-sized fruit. Does well outdoors. Vigorous. |

# 10 Propagation

## Sowing seeds – vegetative propagation – pricking off and potting

Despite its technical sound, the word propagation simply means raising new plants by planting seeds, taking cuttings or dividing up old plants. A greenhouse is far from essential to the propagation process but because its internal atmosphere is protected and controlled it will not only speed up the process but will give you a greater success rating and widen the range of plants that you can multiply to include a whole galaxy of tender and half-hardy species which need the warmth your greenhouse can offer.

Whatever the kind of propagation you have in mind, you must be able to give newly-developing plants air, moisture and the right temperature. There is no infallible method which will bring success. Often trial and error is the quickest way of progress, but there are some general rules which you should stick to.

## Sowing seeds

Growing plants from seed is cheap and gives good results, but do resist the temptation to collect your own seeds from plants you have grown in the greenhouse. Rather, buy from a reputable dealer. The reason for this is that flowers which are fertilized with pollen from another plant may not breed true.

While some seeds, like those of the cucumber, germinate very quickly and easily, others, like primula seeds are very difficult to germinate. One reason for this is a very hard seed coat which acts as a barrier and prevents water reaching the embryo within, another is that the seed may naturally have a long resting or dormancy period. For hard-coated seeds, the best treatment is to dip them into hot water before you plant them, as this will soften them and allow water in. To break the dormancy spell, put the seeds into a refrigerator for a few weeks before taking them into a warm greenhouse.

The best substance to grow seeds in, whatever their size or shape, is U/C or John Innes seed compost, or some other all-peat mix. The container you choose will depend on how many seeds you plan to plant. For small batches use clay or plastic seed 'pans' or bowls, for large ones seed trays are best. Available in wood, plastic or polystyrene, these trays have standard dimensions of $14 \times 9 \times 12$ in. If you plant in old fish boxes, make sure that they are not contaminated with salt. Plastic seed trays are probably the best choice, as they are so simple to clean and do not rot, and these are sometimes attached to polythene covers to make small propagating units.

If you are using a box for planting, fill the bottom with some roughage like rough peat before you add the compost. Clay seed bowls will need some pieces of crock put over the drainage hole. Other containers can be filled directly with the compost. Add it up to the rim, make sure it is warm and damp and press it down with a piece of wood so that the surface is even. Water well and allow it to drain, or stand the container in a shallow tray containing an inch or so of water for a few minutes.

The best way to sow fine seed is to scatter it thinly on the surface then press it in lightly. Hold the container at eye level to make sure of even sowing. Larger seeds can either be scattered over the surface then covered with some more compost rubbed through a fine riddle. A method which has been tried and tested by gardeners for years is to put the seeds into a piece of cardboard folded down the middle. If you prefer to plant with 'finger and thumb', remember that fine seeds will stick to your fingers. Large seeds can merely be pressed into the compost.

Try to sow as thinly as you can and after sowing *always* give seeds a very light watering with a very fine rose. Then cover them with a sheet of glass with paper on top. This keeps the humidity high and traps moisture. Light is unnecessary and often undesirable for germination.

The ideal temperature for germination varies from species to species, but 55–60 °F will suit the majority, though begonias need about 10° more than this. Look at the seed containers often to make sure that they are not dry and turn the glass over every day so that drops of water do not soak the compost. As soon as you see signs of germination, remove the paper and lift the glass a little to let some air in. For the next few days, keep the seedlings out of bright sunlight, even if you have to protect them with a sheet of tissue paper. Finally, if you have the facilities, you might like to imitate the commercial growers and keep the greenhouse at high humidity and a temperature of 75 °F for a few days, in which time, many seeds will germinate.

# Vegetative propagation

As its name suggests, vegetative propagation involves taking off some part of the plant and inducing it to make roots. These cuttings may be from the stem, leaves or the roots themselves, or may be in the form of a bulb, a runner or a tuber. In general, the plants whose roots grow closest to the surface of the ground are easiest to propagate: the chrysanthemum is a good example.

The most favourable time for taking cuttings is the season when the plant is growing most rapidly. For plants with soft wood, like dahlias and chrysanthemums, this will be early in the year when the new season's growth has begun. The cuttings do, however, need high temperatures – between 60 and 65 °F – to form roots.

Pelargoniums, hydrangeas and many other shrubs with moderate amounts of wood are best propagated later in the year. They can be rooted at lower temperatures, that is, from 50 to 55 °F. Woody plants, like roses, give the best cuttings in autumn, and will form roots at low temperatures but the vital rooting process will be speeded up considerably in the warmth of the greenhouse.

Usually, the tips of the side shoots, or sometimes the end of the main growing shoot, make the best cuttings, but do reject any plants which show signs of disease so that your cuttings are as healthy as possible. Snapping the cutting off cleanly by hand will cut down the risk of spreading fungi or viruses, but if you prefer to use a knife choose one with a sharp narrow blade or employ a fairly new razor blade.

The best length for a cutting is 2 or 3 in., though some roses can be propagated from long cuttings bearing three or four buds. Whatever your plant, make sure that you do not bruise either parent or offspring during the propagation. Put the cuttings in boxes, seed pans or open beds which you have filled with a rooting medium. This can be sand, peat, a mixture of the two or one of peat and vermiculite. Or you can use the new peat pellets which do away with the need for transplanting later on. Dib out holes with a pencil, and put the cuttings in 1–3 in. apart, having dusted them, if you wish, with hormone rooting powder, according to the maker's directions.

Two common greenhouse plants, the rex begonias and saintpaulia, are often propagated by taking leaf cuttings. For the begonias, take off a large leaf and make some cuts across the leaf veins then lie it on some rooting compost. Some gardeners put small stones over the cuts, but this is not essential. Take off saintpaulia leaves with a little of the stem attached and simply stand them in the compost. Both these sorts of leaf cuttings thrive in high humidity.

All cuttings will make roots more quickly if you can set up some sort of humid, enclosed atmosphere. This may merely be a polythene bag attached to a stick, or may be a mist propagating unit which carefully controls heat and moisture. Plastic propagating cases, consisting of a tray and a transparent cover are cheap to buy and very effective. Maintain the temperature of the greenhouse at a level which can be kept similar to that of the rooting medium. A figure between 55 and 60 °F is acceptable for most plants.

## Pricking off and potting

Once seedlings are well grown and cuttings obviously rooting and established in the growing medium, both can be transferred or pricked off to boxes or pots of the right size. Do not choose pots that are too large, particularly for cuttings, for contact with the sides of the pot encourages roots to grow. And remember that plants in clay or plastic pots will need re-potting while those in peat or bituminized paper pots can be transplanted in their entirety.

To avoid damaging the leaves or roots, tease seedlings out of their germination trays gently with a dibber. Look at the roots to make sure that they are not diseased – they should be white, not brown – then make a hole in the new medium with your dibber and pop the seedling in. Then firm it up with the dibber base. If you are pricking off into standard boxes, put 8 seedlings per row in six rows and try to have some sort of grading system according to size. If you are using soil blocks, you will have to add extra compost to fill up the indentation. Once they have been planted and firmed in, give a good watering.

Cuttings can be handled very much like seedlings and both must be kept at a favourable temperature of around 60 °F. Many gardeners think that in winter open benches give the plants a better start in life, but a closed-in situation will be better in summer, as the plants will then need less watering.

The time for the next re-potting or for planting out will depend on how quickly the new plants grow and how many roots they make. Moving a plant into a larger pot is quite simple. Choose a pot 2 in. larger in diameter. Put a little roughage in the bottom and partly fill it with compost. Take the small pot containing the plant, turn it upside down and tap the base lightly. Cup the ball of the roots in your hand as the plant comes out so that it does not disintegrate, then put it on the compost layer in the new pot. Fill the pot to within $\frac{1}{2}$ in. of the rim and press in firmly if the plant is shrubby or woody, less firmly if it is soft and sappy. At every stage, take the trouble to label the plants clearly and carefully.

All plants which will eventually flower or fruit outdoors must be gradually accustomed to temperatures outside the greenhouse. This hardening-off process is ideally accomplished in a cold frame, but a sunny, sheltered spot will do. In a frame, give more and more air each day until April or May when there is no chance of a late frost.

Kalanchoës are succulent, greenhouse perennials with fragrant flowers. Many flower from winter to spring, and they can be placed out of doors in summer.

# 11 Diseases, Pests and Other Problems

In the congenial atmosphere of the greenhouse, plants grow quickly, but so too do all kinds of pests and diseases, and the less the greenhouse environment is controlled, the more rampant these pests and diseases will be. This, however, is not the whole answer and yet effective though modern chemical controls can be, many organisms have built up a resistance to these compounds.

Just as the human body is made more vulnerable by the extremes of cold and heat, so greenhouse plants will be attacked more easily if you give them too much or too little food, excess or lack of water, if you overheat the greenhouse or forget to turn the heating on. Hygiene is important, too. Many pests and diseases are so small that they are invisible to the naked eye, but regularly disinfecting your equipment with detergent will control them.

## Warning

If you use chemical pesticides and insecticides, *always* follow the manufacturer's instructions to the letter. Fumigants need particularly careful handling. *Lock all these substances away* out of the reach of children. The chemical DDT is often referred to in gardening books but is no longer available as it has been judged injurious to man and animals. Finally, the chemicals referred to in the tables which follow are listed either in the Agricultural Chemicals Approval Scheme Booklet *Chemicals for the Gardener* or in *Approved Products for Farmers*, but new chemicals for controlling pests and diseases are, of course, constantly coming on the market.

# Pests, Diseases and Problems

| CROP, PLANT OR GREENHOUSE | DISORDERS | SYMPTOMS | PREVENTION AND CONTROL |
|---|---|---|---|
| General propagation, seed sowing, rooting cuttings, culture of young plants, bedding plants, etc. | Damping off; Pythium Spp.; Rhizoctonia Spp., Phytophthora Spp | Base of seedlings and young plants turns light brown and stem constricts. Plant eventually collapses. Cuttings attacked in area of cut part or at compost level. | Cheshunt compound can be used before sowing and also for newly-germinated seedlings. Zineb or quintozene (PCNB) can also be used, as instructed on product, as can captan dust or spray |
| General propagation, seed sowing, rooting cuttings, culture of young plants, bedding plants, etc. | Grey mould | Attacks cuttings or young plants. Starts as light brown lesion, eventually becoming covered with grey dust-like spores | Again encouraged by high humidity. Especially troublesome in a greenhouse which is allowed to chill overnight. Use Thiram dust as directed on product, Captan or Tecnazene dust |
| Bulbs and corms; Carnations, chrysanthemums, cucumbers, pot plants, tomatoes, lettuce, peaches, nectarines, and crops in general | Aphids of various species. Small flies can be seen on leaves, usually in clusters | Attack leaves, feeding on plant sap, causing distortion and loss of vigour Virus disease can also be transmitted by various species | Use insecticidal spray or atomizing fluid or smoke at first sign of attack, changing the nature of the chemical frequently, if possible, to avoid build up of resistance. Malathion, nicotine, derris gamma BHC, Dimethcate, Formothion, Menazon, are the main chemicals used. The last three are all systemics |
| Bulbs and corms; chrysanthemums, tomatoes, and several other crops | Caterpillars; Angle shade moth; Tomato moth | Caterpillars feeding on leaves and flowers, often at night | Gamma BHC smokes and sprays Cabaryl Fenitrothion and Trichlorphon sprays |
| Bulbs and corms; chrysanthemums | Stem eelworm (Ditylenchus dipsaci) attacks bulbs and other plants. Chrysanthemums attacked by specific eelworm (Apelenchoides ritzems-bosi) | Attack leaves and flowers causing distortion. In chrysanthemums brown blotches are formed on leaves, changing from yellow to bronze and purple | Destroy stock of bulbs and use only fresh soil in future. Chrysanthemums stools can be hot water treated – 115°F. for 5 minutes |
| Narcissus (daffodils) | Narcissus flies | Eggs laid in or near bulbs in spring. Produce larvae which tunnel into bulbs, resulting in failure after planting | Bulb suppliers generally ensure that all blubs are free from infestation by hot water treatment or chemical dipping |

| CROP, PLANT OR GREENHOUSE | DISORDERS | SYMPTOMS | PREVENTION AND CONTROL |
|---|---|---|---|
| Narcissus (daffodils) | Leaf scorch (Stagonospora curtisii) | Leaf tip turns reddish brown, followed by death | Spray with Zineb at first sign of attack and repeat several times |
| Bulbs and corms; Carnations, chrysanthemums, cucumbers, pot plants generally, tomatoes, inside shrubs | Thrips of various species, small brown or yellowish insects | Attack plants in various ways – sucking sap from leaves or flowers, causing acute distortion of growth. Silvery spots often show, especially on carnations. Breeding is more or less continuous | BHC smoke varied with Derris, Malathion and Nicotine, applied repeatedly until control is gained |
| Carnations, chrysanthemums, lettuce, tomatoes | Wireworms (small $\frac{1}{2}$–$\frac{3}{4}$ in. yellow-bodied insects) | Eggs laid in May/July. Larvae hatch in a few weeks and eat roots of plants. Persist for 4–5 years | Apply BHC (Gamma) as soil dust |
| Carnations, tomatoes | Fusarium wilt (Fusarium oxysporum and F. dianthi and other species) | Carnations and tomatoes are affected in warm areas. Plant wilt badly | Use clean stock and sterilized soil. Use Zineb when disease first appears |
| All crops | Grey mould (Botrytis cinerea) | Attacks a wide range of plants, causing discoloration of leaves, followed by grey dust-like mould. Spreads extremely rapidly. Tomatoes badly attacked on stems, leaves or fruit. Ghost spot on fruit is caused by partial development of botrytis. Lettuce can also be badly attacked | Keep atmosphere dry by skilful ventilation and application of heat. Avoid severe night temperature drops. Thiram dust or TCNB smoke should be used with care according to directions. Alternatively use Dicloran, Zineb or Benomyl (systemic) |
| Carnations | Carnation fly | Eggs laid on upper surface of leaves, resulting in larvae which moves into the stem | BHC smokes and sprays |
| Tulips | 'Fire' (Botrytis tulipae) | Deformed shoots, followed by grey spots which eventually run together, resulting in reddish discoloration of leaves | Zineb, Thiram or Quintozene (PCNB) sprays or dust used at first sign of attack and persisted with |
| Many crops and plants | Earwigs | Bite holes in flowers and stems during night, causing acute distortion and malformation | Trap with inverted pots, and spray or dust with Gamma BHC |

| Host | Pest/Disease | Description | Control |
|---|---|---|---|
| Many crops and plants | Red Spider Mite (Tetranychus urticae and T. cinnebarinus) | Nymphs and adults suck sap from leaves, causing yellowing and eventual destruction of leaves. Webs develop on underside of leaves, hindering control | Extremely persistent pests, over-wintering in cracks in greenhouse. A variety of materials should be used as smokes or sprays to avoid building up resistance. These include azo-benzene, derris, petroleum oil, Malathion and pormothion |
| Carnations, chrysanthemums, pot plants and shrubs | Powdery mildew (Oidium sp.) | Dirty white powder on leaves, stems and flowers | Dinocap spray or dust at first sign of attack |
| Carnations, chrysanthemums, and other plants | Rust (Uromyces dianthi) | Small blotches on leaves, later releasing reddish brown spores | Thiram, Zineb sprays or dusts, at first sign of disease. Overwinters in stools of chrysanthemums |
| Carnations | Stem rot (Fusarium culmorum) Verticillium wilt (Verticillium cinerescens) | Soil borne disease enters roots and spreads up plant, affecting moisture conducting tissue. Wilt follows, sometimes only on one side of plant on carnations | Adequate soil sterilization by heat or effective chemicals. Raising greenhouse temperature to 75 °F. for a week, combined with surface mulching, can offset trouble. Watering with Zineb is reasonably effective |
| Tomatoes | Verticillium wilt (Verticillium albaatrum) | | |
| Chrysanthemums | Gall midge (Diarthronomyia chrysanthemi) | Cone-shaped galls form on leaves and stems | Spray with gamma BHC at first sign of attack |
| Chrysanthemums, lettuce | Stool miner (Palla nigricornis) | Larvae feed on stem base and destroy cutting material | Spray with gamma BHC or Trichlophon spring and summer to destroy eggs. Lift and destroy all affected stools. With lettuce use Gamma BHC before planting after an attack, on a previous crop |
| Chrysanthemums, pot plants, tomatoes | Leaf miner (Phytomyza and Liriomyza solani) | Eggs laid on leaves produce larvae which tunnel into leaves | Gamma BHC aerosol, Gamma BHC smoke, when attack first noticed, or Trichlophon spray |
| Chrysanthemums | Tarnished plant bug or capsid (Lygus rugulipennis) | Bugs suck sap, exuding toxin which twists and distorts. A wide range of plants are attacked out of doors. | Malathion sprays, Gamma BHC smokes or sprays and Fenitrothion sprays |
| Chrysanthemums, cucumbers, melons, pot plants, tomatoes | White Fly (Trialeurodes vaporariorum) | Eggs laid on leaves, hatching into nymphs which suck sap and exude honeydew on which moulds develop. Growth is distorted. In pelargoniums leaf spot may be spread by this pest | A variety of sprays, dusts, aerosols, or smokes can be used, based on, Gamma BHC, Malathion, Pyrethrum or Derris. All must be used within 14 days and at short intervals to ensure control. Thorough cleaning or fumigating of greenhouse in winter when empty is essential |

| CROP, PLANT OR GREENHOUSE | DISORDERS | SYMPTOMS | PREVENTION AND CONTROL |
|---|---|---|---|
| Chrysanthemums | Blotch or leaf spot (Spetoria chrysanthemella) | Grey or black blotches on leaves, often confused with eelworm | Spray with Zineb |
| Chrysanthemums | Petal damping, botrytis, grey mould | 'Pin-pointing' of flower, followed by complete flower rot | Improve environment by application of heat, especially at night. TCNB smoke can be used at first sign of attack |
| Chrysanthemums | Petal blight (Itersonilia spp.) | Affects outside petals as water spots and spreads into flower centre | Zineb spray or dust before bud bursting |
| Chrysanthemums | Ray blight (Mycosphaerella ligulicola) | Mainly attacks inside when growing chrysanthemums on year round culture | Obtain clean stock. Spray with Zineb. Difficult to control once in existence |
| Cucumber | French fly (Tyrophagus sp.) | Introduced on straw (bales or loose). Mites feed on growing plant and leaves causing pale spots which later develop into holes. Usually disappear in high summer | Nicotine smokes or sprays |
| Cucumbers, melons, tomatoes | Leaf hoppers (Erythroneura pallidifrons) | Lively insects feeding on leaves cause distortion and restrict growth | Nicotine, malathion or Fenuitrothion at first sign of attack |
| Cucumber | Fungus gnats of various species | Develop initially on decaying fungi, FYM, or straw bales. Attack roots of plants causing wilting or death | Malathion watered into bed or use Gamma BHC drench |
| Cucumbers, melons and other soft plants | Springtails of various species | White six-legged soil pests feeding on soft stems, roots and root hairs in clusters. Some actively jump by means of tails | Gamma BHC drenches or dusts |
| Cucumbers, melons, lettuce, tomatoes and practically all other plants | Symphylid (Scutigerella immaculata) | Very active $\frac{1}{4}$ in. long insects feeding on roots, causing hard or deformed growth. They move down to lower depths of soil in winter or when soil is wet. Worst in highly organic soil | Thoroughly sterilize soil by heat or effective chemicals, Malathion drenches can be reasonably effective |
| Cucumbers, tomatoes and other plants | Woodlice of various species | Attack plant roots or stems at soil level with drastic effects if in large numbers | Bait with cut turnips, Gamma BHC |
| Cucumbers | Black rot (Mycosphaerella citrullina) | Dieback of laterals at main stem. Identified by small black spots | Zineb spray, coupled with sterilization of boxes, etc. to avoid spread of infection |